# Singing of the
Source

A publication of the
SCHOOL OF HAWAIIAN
ASIAN & PACIFIC STUDIES
University of Hawaii

# Singing of the Source

## Nature and God in the Poetry of the Chinese Painter Wu Li

Jonathan Chaves

*SHAPS Library of Translations*
*University of Hawaii Press / Honolulu*

98 97 96 95 94 93   5 4 3 2 1

**Library of Congress Cataloging-in-Publication Data**

Chaves, Jonathan.

    Singing of the source : nature and god in the poetry of the

Chinese painter Wu Li / Jonathan Chaves.

      p.   cm.

    Includes bibliographical references and index.

    ISBN 0–8248–1485–1 (acid-free)

    1. Wu, Li, 1632–1718—Criticism and interpretation.  2. Wu, Li,

1632–1718—Religion.  I. Title.

PL2732.U2337Z6   1993

895.1′148—dc20                        93–3878

                                              CIP

*Designed by Kenneth Miyamoto*

*To Ian, Colin, and Rachel*

That love, life, and work may be one

For if I should (said he)
Bestow this jewel also on my creature,
He would adore my gifts instead of me,
And rest in Nature, not the God of Nature:
   So both should losers be.

—George Herbert, "The Pulley"


The shelves are full, all other themes are sped;
Hackney'd and worn to the last flimsy thread. . . .
And 'tis the sad complaint, and almost true,
Whate'er we write, we bring forth nothing new.
'Twere new indeed to see a bard all fire,
Touch'd with a coal from Heaven, assume the lyre. . . .

—William Cowper, "Table Talk"

# Contents

# Preface

This book has two purposes. It is the first comprehensive study and presentation in any language of the poetry of Wu Li, a man famous as one of the orthodox masters of early Ch'ing-dynasty painting, but whose very reputation as a painter even in his own lifetime obscured his achievement as a poet. And the book is an attempt to come to grips with the role played by Christianity in seventeenth-century China as embodied in the personal conversion experience of one individual: Wu Li.

Increasing attention to poetry of the later era—the Yüan, Ming, and Ch'ing dynasties—is one of the salient developments in recent Chinese poetry studies. I myself have striven to contribute to this exciting new field in a series of articles on individual poets of the Ming–Ch'ing transition, which has emerged through recent scholarship as a particularly fascinating period of ferment in both poetry and painting, as well as in my *Columbia Book of Later Chinese Poetry* (1986). For each of the early Ch'ing poets I have studied—Wu Chia-chi (1618–1684), Ch'ien Ch'ien-i (1582–1664), and now, Ch'ien's pupil in poetry, Wu Li (1632–1718)—I have aimed at showing that while the individual poet may have been drawing from aspects of the past, he was unmistakably original in the variations he rang upon some traditional theme.

Wu Li is here presented as a participant in the rediscovery of Sung-dynasty poetry and poetics in the early Ch'ing, centering on the publication in 1671 of *Sung-shih ch'ao* by Wu Chih-chen (1640–1717) and his colleagues. I shall demonstrate that Wu Li was associated, however briefly, with the circle of important poets and scholars who enjoyed first access to this major compilation of Sung poetry, and that he was influenced by Sung poetry to produce a highly accomplished body of conventional poetry in what might be called a neo-Sung manner. But his real originality, I argue, lies in the unprecedented boldness of his experimental creation: a Chinese Christian poetry, a poetry utterly traditional in its use of *shih* and *ch'ü* forms and such devices as parallelism and allusion, but equally *un*conventional in being based on orthodox Christian theology.

The conversion experience which led Wu Li to become a member of the Jesuit society, and eventually to be ordained as one of the first Chinese Catholic priests, is explored here in the context of widespread intellectual and spiritual ferment in the early Ch'ing, as well as considerable conversion activity among the various religions of China, especially conversions from Confucianism to Buddhism, in the wake of the collapse of the Ming dynasty. Nevertheless, the conversion of Wu Li is ultimately taken to be an authentic non-coerced spiritual experience irreducible to social, economic, or even psychological determinants either singly or in combination. The enormous leap by which a Chinese scholar deeply immersed, as will be seen, in Neo-Confucianism and Buddhism would seek to become a Christian, and would then be inspired to compose Christian poetry in classical Chinese poetic forms, is the central mystery which this book hopes, not to explain completely, but to elucidate to some degree.

# Abbreviations

CKH: Chou K'ang-hsieh 周康燮, ed. *Wu Yü-shan yen-chiu lun-chi* 吳漁山研究論集. Hong Kong: Ch'ung-wen Bookstore, 1971.

MCC: Li Ti, S.J. 李杕, ed. *Mo-ching chi* 墨井集. Shanghai: Hsü-chia-hui 徐家滙 ("Zikawei") Press, 1909. The copy of this rare book I consulted is in the East Asian Library at Washington University in St. Louis.

MCSC: *Mo-ching shih-ch'ao* 墨井詩鈔. In Ku Hsiang 顧湘, ed., *Hsiao-shih shan-fang ts'ung-shu* 小石山房叢書, 1874; and MCC, chap. 2.

# The Poet

# 1

# *Wu Li's Literary World*

Wu Li is a familiar figure to students of Chinese painting. Together with Yün Shou-p'ing 惲壽平 (1633–1690), Wang Shih-min 王時敏 (1592–1680), Wang Chien 王鑑 (1598–1677), Wang Hui 王翬 (1632–1717), and Wang Yüan-ch'i 王原祁 (1642–1715), he is classified as one of the Six Orthodox Masters of early Ch'ing-dynasty painting. Some attention has also been given to his conversion at an uncertain date to Catholicism, entry into the Society of Jesus in 1682, and ordination as a priest in 1688. But his poetry has gone largely unstudied, with the exceptions of references in an article on Wu (1936) and a *nien-p'u* 年譜 on him (1937) by Ch'en Yüan 陳垣,[1] and annotations to certain individual poems of Wu's by Fang Hao 方豪 (1950 and after) and Wang Tsung-yen 汪宗衍 (1971).[2] Nevertheless, the modern anthologist Teng Chih-ch'eng 鄧之誠, in editing his *Ch'ing-shih chi-shih ch'u-pien* 清詩紀事初編 (1965), thought highly enough of Wu Li's poetry to include three of his poems and a brief essay on Wu as poet.[3] After noting that Wu Li studied poetry under Ch'ien Ch'ien-i 錢謙益 (1582–1664) and painting under Wang Shih-min (facts recorded, as Teng notes, in a biography of Wu by a certain Chang Yün-chang 張雲章 of Chia-ting 嘉定 dating from 1714),[4] Teng concludes his essay by stating:

> Li's poetry has been obscured by his fame in painting, and his personal character has been obscured by his poetry and painting. Those who praise Li today also stress his transmission of religion, but how can they understand that in those days, when he entered the Way, it was because of having undergone bitterness and suffering which cannot be explained to people?

In using the expression *shih wei hua-ming so yen* 詩為畫名所掩 ("his poetry has been obscured by his fame in painting"), Teng may be hearkening back to a comment on the great painter-poet Shen Chou 沈周 (1427–1509) rendered by the scholar Ho Liang-chün 何良俊 (1506–1573) and echoed through the centuries in later evaluations of the reputations of painter-poets: "Some of Shih-t'ien's 石田 [Shen Chou's] poems are outstandingly fine, but they have been obscured by his painting and so the world does not praise them" (石田詩有絕佳者,但為畫所掩,世不之稱).[5] More immediately, Teng may have had in mind the echo of Ho's phrase in the last of the four prefaces to the 1719 edition of Wu Li's poetry known as *Mo-ching shih-ch'ao* 墨井詩鈔, the one written by Yü Huai 余懷 (1616–1696),[6] in which Yü laments: "People only know that he is good at painting, but they do not know of his skill at poetry; people only know that his poetry has been obscured by his painting (其詩以畫掩), but they do not realize that his painting has been transmitted because of his poetry." (The final part of this statement is clearly hyperbolic, but in the first part Yü at one stroke suggests that even in Wu's day he was better known as a painter than as a poet, and that there was a consensus, presumably among his admirers, that his poetry was unjustly neglected.)

The highest praise yet accorded to Wu Li's poetry has come from Albert Chan, S.J., who writes: "His poems are graceful and limpid, especially those of his later years, which couch Catholic thought in exquisite style; he was perhaps the first in China to find a poetic vehicle for Christian doctrine. His poems manifest his devout life and his admiration for the scientific achievements of the early Jesuits."[7]

## Wu Li's Reputation as a Poet

In Wu Li's own day, those like Yü Huai who did praise his poetry seem inevitably to have done so in a context which emphasizes that he was, after all, primarily a painter. Wu's painting teacher, Wang Shih-min, in a colophon "Inscribed at the End of Wu Yü-shan's [Wu Li's] Poem and Painting, 'Suffering from the Rain,'"[8] writes:

[Wu Li] is skillful at poetry and at the same time excellent at the matter of painting. With Censor Hsü Ch'ing-yü of P'i-ling he has established a relationship of literature—brush and ink—and there is no disagreement in their views. They often travel to see famous sights; ornamented carriage and rowed boat they never fail to share. They exchange poems and essays and in the course of time these have formed a volume. Recently [Wu Li] also has written a sixteen-line poem, "Sighing Over the Rain," which he has connected to a painting, and this can be considered a particularly suitable match [between the two arts].[9] . . . "Painting in poetry, poetry in painting": in this scroll they are fully complete. When it comes to the Way of poetry, I am at a loss; how would I dare rashly to "insert my beak" even the least bit? But when I gaze from two hundred *li* away, I see the tones of the Great Elegance *Ta ya* 大雅 produced by great men and noble scholars, "very grand," "extensive and lovely,"[10] mutually illuminating the precious picture, a fine episode for the Garden of Art. . . .

The "Hsü Ch'ing-yü" referred to by Wang Shih-min is Wu Li's closest friend in the 1670s, Hsü Chih-chien 許之漸 (*chin-shih*, 1655), a figure known in the history of Catholicism in China because of the anti-Catholic polemic launched against him by Yang Kuang-hsien 楊光先 (1597–1669).[11] As Ch'en Yüan has noted,[12] there are indeed a number of poems in MCSC addressed to him, and he figures importantly in the colophons of a number of Wu Li's paintings, including the handscroll of 1679 entitled "Whiling Away the Summer at the Inkwell Thatched Hut" (*Mo-ching ts'ao-t'ang hsiao-hsia t'u* 墨井草堂消夏圖), now in the Metropolitan Museum of Art in New York, which is dedicated to him, although Ch'en rejects the claim in one of the later colophons to this scroll that Hsü like Wu converted to Catholicism. (A detail from this painting is reproduced here as Plate 2.)

Wang Shih-min's chief concern seems to be to present Wu Li as a traditional *wen-jen* 文人 literatus, exchanging poems with a "friend in poetry," as did Po Chü-i 白居易 (772–846) and Yüan Chen 元稹 (779–831), or Lu Kuei-meng 陸龜蒙 (d. ca. 881) and P'i Jih-hsiu 皮日休 (ca. 833–883), or Mei Yao-ch'en 梅堯臣 (1002–

1060) and Ou-yang Hsiu 歐陽修 (1007–1072). Still, the close connection of his poetry with his painting remains fundamental in the colophon.

One might expect Wu's painting master to emphasize his painting, but even his poetry master, Ch'ien Ch'ien-i, in a colophon (or preface) to an early collection of Wu's poetry—*T'ao-ch'i shih-kao* 桃溪詩稿,[13] now apparently lost as an independent book, although some or all of the poems in it were probably edited into MCSC—if anything places more stress on Wu's painting than Wang Shih-min does. Only after a lengthy discussion of the influence on Wu of certain great painters, in which he praises Wu's ability in the depiction of architectural elements and human figures, as well as his painstaking application of "texture-strokes" (*ts'un* 皴) and washes, does Ch'ien so much as mention Wu's poetry—even though the text in question is supposedly about his poetry collection in the first place. When Ch'ien does finally get around to the poetry, he writes:

> Yü-shan is not only good at painting; he is exceptionally skill-ful at poetry. The thought [in his poems] is pure and the style ancient. In his command of the brush he achieves the subtle. For this too [the writing of poetry] he does on the basis of his painting: he does not wish to vie in prettiness with the world of fashion [in poetry and painting] by smearing rouge and daubing powder.

Ch'ien then returns to the discussion of painting as such, which he maintains to the end, although he states at one point that, "of course, there has never been a scholar of whom it could be said that he was a good painter even though he did not draw upon the well-water of antiquity or work at literature." Ch'ien also speaks of Wu Li as a "Huang [Kung-wang] or Shen [Chou] of our time." Huang Kung-wang 黃公望 (1269–1354) was one of the Four Masters of Yüan-dynasty painting. Shen Chou, as we have seen, had a reputation both as painter and poet.

In a different context—a eulogy on Wu Li's mother written by Ch'ien at Wu's request—Ch'ien does end the brief preface with the statement, "Her youngest son, Li, can write poetry and has a reputation (能詩有聞). He has asked me to write a eulogy for her."[14] It is unclear from the wording whether Wu Li's "reputation" was specifically for his ability at writing poetry. No mention is made of his painting, but as a eulogy on one's mother would be a highly formal text, reference to what was officially regarded as a somewhat frivolous pastime might have been considered inappropriate.

When MCSC was edited in 1719 (the year after Wu Li's death), four prefaces were printed along with it. All four of them treat Wu Li as primarily a painter, even though with some regrets at the neglect of his poetry. The first, dated 1668, is by a certain T'ang Yü-chao 唐宇昭 (the second character of his name also appears as Yü 于 or even Yü 禹).[15] T'ang, known for his *ch'uan-ch'i* 傳奇 plays and for his forty poems "In Imitation of Palace Lyrics" (*ni kung-tz'u* 擬宮詞),[16] tells how he "had long heard of Yü-shan's name, but had not yet seen his painting." Only later did he discover Wu Li's character; and last of all his poetry:

> Yü-shan is not a man typical of the present time. And so I asked to see his paintings. His paintings are not of a single style. Some are landscapes, some human figures or flowers and birds. . . . Next I sought out the poems in his book-basket. They were all in the form of little fascicles [*chih* 帙], and the fascicles made up more than a single anthology [*chi* 集]. He happened to show me the Peach Stream Anthology [*T'ao-ch'i chi*], the one Mu-weng [Ch'ien Ch'ien-i] had enjoyed greatly and discussed with words of praise.

T'ang also says that he spoke about Wu Li to Hsü Chih-chien, and it was Hsü who had the idea that T'ang write this preface, originally intended for the *T'ao-ch'i* anthology, four years after the death of Ch'ien Ch'ien-i.[17]

The second preface to MCSC, the most intellectually interesting of the four, is by Ch'en Yü-chi 陳玉璂 (chin-shih, 1667), the son-in-law of Wu's friend Hsü Chih-chien and a scholar with a reputation both for prose and for poetry, who was anthologized in *Ch'ing-shih chi-shih* (although the editor, Teng Chih-ch'eng, says his prose is superior to his poetry, which is not his forte) and in *Ch'ing-shih pieh-ts'ai chi* 清詩別裁集, edited by Shen Te-ch'ien 沈德潛 (1673–1769) and others.[18] Ch'en develops a distinction between those "men of today who make it their rule to imitate the poems of men of the past, carving their hearts and puncturing their reins to seek skillfulness, and yet in the end they are not skillful," and those who "happen to see some scenes or phenomena between heaven and earth, enjoyable or detestable, and upon contact with them form poems, and their skillfulness ends up superior to that of the ancients." This may be seen as a reference to the ortho-dox masters of the Ming and their emphasis on imitation of the great writers of the past, as opposed to the individualists of the Kung-an school and the concept of direct experience leading to naturalness of expression. Wu Li is enlisted by Ch'en on the side of those who "master it without intention" (*wu hsin erh te chih* 無心而得之), but only after a somewhat turgid attempt to argue that painters, by contrast with poets, need not experience the phe-nomena of the world directly because they already contain them "within the breast," so that they can "close their eyes and engage in meditative viewing [*ming-shih* 冥視], and then that which they contact within the breast will be plentiful." Perhaps this argument is intended as a kind of compliment to Wu Li, for Ch'en continues:

> Master Wu Yü-shan is famous as a painter. He is also skilled at poetry. His poetry entirely does away with the practice of "carving and weaving"; he follows the self-so. Chung Jung 鍾嶸 [ca. 465–518] says that T'ao Yüan-ming's [T'ao Ch'ien 陶潛 (365–427)] poetry "emerged from that of Ying Chü 應璩."[19] I say Yü-shan's poetry in fact emerged from Yüan-ming, and yet Yü-shan simply lets flow directly the scenes and phenomena in his breast. When has he ever depended upon a man of former times?

Ch'en Yü-chi, in associating Wu Li with a natural, direct mode of expression derived in a sense from T'ao Ch'ien, is in fact linking him with the whole movement away from T'ang-oriented archaism to a new appreciation for Sung poetry and its characteristic under-stated manner; we shall shortly see that Wu Li was indeed in-fluenced by this movement. Ch'en Yü-chi was an insightful critic who also wrote prefaces to the poetry of such major figures of the day as Wu Wei-yeh 吳偉業 (1609–1672), Wang Shih-chen 王士禎 (1634–1711), and Shih Jun-chang 施閏章 (1619–1683),[20] with all of whom Wu Li too had some contact. (It remains unclear whether he actually met Wu Wei-yeh.)[21]

The third preface to MCSC is by none other than Ch'en Hu 陳瑚 (1613–1675),[22] who, as Chang Yün-chang points out in his biography, was Wu Li's teacher in Confucian philosophy and indeed, as we shall see, a leading Confucian thinker of his time. He describes Wu Li as a master of the *ch'in* 琴 zither and a calligrapher, but then goes on like the other preface writers to remind us that he "was exceptionally good at painting landscapes." After quoting at some length from Ch'ien Ch'ien-i's colophon-preface to Wu's *T'ao-ch'i shih-kao,* he notes that "Tsung-po [Ch'ien Ch'ien-i], in prefacing Wu's poetry, simultaneously brought in his painting to this degree," making the point we have been establishing— namely, that those who praise Wu Li's poetry always stress the primacy of his painting or at least mention the fact of his being a painter. Ch'en Hu then names Wang Wei 王維 (701–761), Shen Chou, and Wen Cheng-ming 文徵明 (1470–1559) as rare examples from earlier periods of men who combined poetry and painting like Wu Li.

Finally, as we have seen, Yü Huai, a writer with a reputation for his *tz'u* 詞 poetry and for his memoirs of Nanking, *Pan-ch'iao tsa-chi* 板橋雜記—which contain, as Strassberg notes, "intimate accounts of the personalities and manners of the pleasure quarters,"[23] including the biographies of various famed singing girls—in the fourth and last preface to MCSC expresses regret that Wu Li's fame as a painter prevented recognition of his poetry.[24] Yü Huai refers to another apparently lost anthology of Wu's poetry, the *Hsieh-yu chi* 寫憂集.

If the very men who set out to praise Wu Li's poetry found the intimidating effect of his reputation as a painter impossible to ignore, what justification is there today for attempting to focus attention on the poetry? If Wu Li had written only the sort of poetry found in the MCSC, the answer would probably be: very little. But as Albert Chan's statement cited above makes clear, Wu Li was to write an entirely different sort of poetry in his later years. He was to attempt, in fact, the creation of something completely unprecedented in the history of Chinese poetry, something justifying Ch'en Yü-chi's claim that Wu Li "never depended upon a man of former times" to a degree probably unsuspected by Ch'en himself—a Chinese Christian poetry. This attempt, whether aesthetically successful or not, must be considered one of the boldest experiments in Chinese literary history. The only comparable project in the past would have been the creation of a Chinese *Buddhist* poetry in the Six Dynasties period, and the problems faced were similar in certain respects: fitting into lines of classical verse new terms, sometimes in awkward polysyllabic transliterated forms, conveying completely new subject matter and ideas. Two broad areas must be examined in determining how Wu Li was able to undertake such a daunting task: the poetic and the intellectual-religious influences that came to bear upon him.

## Wu Li's Early Development as a Poet

Wu's teacher in poetry, according to Chang Yün-chang, was Ch'ien Ch'ien-i, certainly a leading arbiter of literary taste in the early Ch'ing dynasty. Ch'ien, like all early-Ch'ing critics, found himself confronted by the unresolved debate between the Former Seven and Latter Seven Masters of Ming literature—with their emphasis on imitation of the great High T'ang poets, especially Tu Fu 杜甫 (712–770), so as to reach through them to underlying natural principles of composition—and the Individualists, especially the Kung-an 公安 school. As I have written elsewhere:

> Ch'ien disliked the orthodox Masters, although he agreed with them that Tu Fu was in fact the supreme poet. He was also suspicious of the Kung-an school, which represented in one aspect a movement to rehabilitate the reputation of Sung poetry, although he shared their admiration for the best Sung poets, especially Su Shih 蘇軾 (1037–1101). . . . On the theoretical level, whatever his professed opinion of the Kung-an school, Ch'ien actually echoes their theory in calling for individuality of style, and even uses their key term, *hsing-ling* 性靈 ("native sensibility" in James J. Y. Liu's translation).[25]

And yet at the same time it is certainly true, as Irving Yucheng Lo and William Schultz write, that Ch'ien's poetry itself demonstrates a heavy "reliance on the use of allusions."[26] How much of this complex—perhaps "eclectic" would be a better word—mix of characteristics Ch'ien passed on to Wu Li is a moot question. Wu Li himself has left us no statements on poetics or on his experience as a student of Ch'ien's—which indeed may not have been extensive.

Probably the most important period in Wu's formation as a poet was during the years 1670–1671, when he was in the capital with Hsü Chih-chien who had been recalled there after a period of banishment brought about by Yang Kuang-hsien's attack on the preface he had supposedly written for the *T'ien-hsüeh ch'uan-kai*. As Ch'en Yüan has demonstrated,[27] Wu Li while in Peking gained admittance to the leading poetic circle of the day, gathered around Wang Shih-chen, and also including such figures as Shih Jun-chang, Sung Wan 宋琬 (1614–1673), and Ch'eng K'o-tse 程可則 (1624–1673). All these men wrote poems to Wu Li—without exception dealing only with his painting.[28] No mention is made in any of them of his poetry. (An apparent comparison of Wu with Hsieh Ling-yün 謝靈運 (385–433) in the Sung Wan poem actually compares with Hsieh the poetry of a certain Hsü Tsuan-tseng 許纘曾, to whom Wu Li had presented a painting as a farewell gift, as Ch'en Yüan has shown.)[29] Shih Jun-chang also wrote a preface to the collected poetry of Wu's friend, Hsü Chih-chien, in which he describes their friendship: "Every day he and his friend Wu Yü-shan take mutual pleasure in literature and wine, roaming freely among ministers and old worthies. . . ."[30]

As a typical example of these poems, here is one by Wang Shih-chen:

> Wu Li's Painting, *My Hut Among Tall Bamboo*
> —Inscribed for the Drafter,
> Wang Chi-chüeh 汪季角

You read books beneath thatched eaves,
  more pleasant than answering the Dynasty's call!
Along the gully, clear shallows flow;
  behind the house, shadows of towering beauty.
I wish to ask that man of Wang-ch'uan:
  does this place compare to the Ridge of Frost-White Bamboo?

Wang Chi-chüeh is Wang Mou-lin 汪懋麟 (1640–1688; the second character of his *tzu* is sometimes written *lu* 甪 or *yung* 用), a poet and disciple of Wang Shih-chen. The "man of Wang-ch'uan" was Wang Wei, the poet-painter to whom Ch'en Hu compares Wu Li in his preface to MCSC, but also Wang Shih-chen's favorite poet—the one he felt best embodied the quality he considered most important in poetic style, *shen-yün* 神韻, or "spirit-resonance," described by James J. Y. Liu as "an ineffable personal tone or flavor in one's poetry."[31] (As the poem Wang Wei wrote on the "Ridge of Frost-White Bamboo" happens to contain the expression *t'an-luan* 檀欒, "towering beauty," Wang Shih-chen's poem is at once an "hommage à Wang Wei" based on a careful reading of his work and a high compliment to Wu Li through implied comparison with Wang Wei.) Wang Shih-chen was, in fact, the leader of the school of poetry termed "metaphysical" by James J. Y. Liu, and looked, as did the orthodox masters, to the High T'ang for his primary inspiration, but he preferred the quiet, exquisitely understated landscape vignettes of Wang Wei to the large-scale works of Tu Fu and Li Po 李白 (701–762). For him, as Lo and Schultz put it, "the essence of poetry is spiritual enlightenment, or a sudden awakening, as taught by the Ch'an (Zen) school of Buddhism."[32] Again, it is difficult to gauge the extent of Wang Shih-chen's influence on Wu Li during his stay in the capital. But Wu may have learned from him or his writings the quasi-religious "metaphysical" conception of poetry.

It may also be through the Wang Shih-chen circle that Wu Li came in contact with a new anthology, printed in 1671, called *Sung-shih ch'ao* 宋詩鈔,[33] and edited by Wu Chih-chen 吳之振 (1640–1717), Lü Liu-liang 呂留良 (1629–1683), and Wu Tzu-mu 吳自牧. This massive anthology—really a collection of lengthy anthologies of the works of individual Sung poets introduced by biographical accounts of the poets written by Lü Liu-liang—was responsible for stimulating the renewed interest in Sung poetry characteristic of the time. Wu Chih-chen, the chief compiler and author of the influential preface, was himself a fine poet, and he knew and admired the poetry of the Wang Shih-chen circle. He wrote two poems after reading Sung Wan's collected works,[34] for example, and sent them to Sung. The terms which Wu employs to describe Sung's poetry are not merely conventional praise but indicate the extent of his own immersion in Sung-dynasty poetry and poetics. The second of these poems is translated here in full:

> In the Hall of Tranquil Elegance [Sung's studio],
>     a single scroll of poems;
> free and easy, rich and full, this man is my teacher!
> He's driven out the clumsy lines
>     of men like Wang and Li;
> cast aside the sleep-talk drivel
>     of Chung and T'an as well.
> Pure, exalted, from the *wu-t'ung* tree
>     autumn dew descends;
> sparse and sere, a pale mist veils willow trees.
> This standard of description is truly hard to reach:
> a book of true prescriptions, doctor to cure vulgarity!

True to his role as champion of Sung poetry, Wu Chih-chen commends Sung Wan for having rejected the style of such orthodox masters as "Wang and Li"—probably Wang Shih-chen 王世貞 (1526–1590) and Li P'an-lung 李攀龍 (1514–1570), the leaders of the Latter Seven Masters—but also for having "cast aside" Chung Hsing 鍾惺 (1574–1624) and T'an Yüan-ch'un 譚元春 (ca. 1585–1637), leaders of the bizarre Ching-ling 竟陵 school often regarded as an offshoot of the Kung-an school but in fact characterized by some of the most awkward diction in all of Chinese poetry. Like Ch'ien Ch'ien-i, Wu Chih-chen may be seen as rejecting *all* of Ming poetry, whatever the school, but he goes much further than Ch'ien in upholding Sung aesthetic values such as *tan* 淡 ("pale," "bland"), used as an adjective here in line 6 modifying the mist in a nature image calculated to evoke the atmosphere of Sung Wan's poetry but well known as the paradoxical aesthetic quality of "blandness" called for by Mei Yao-ch'en and later to become the key concept in Sung aesthetics.[35] It was also Mei Yao-ch'en, as quoted by Ou-yang Hsiu in his *Liu-i shih-hua* 六一詩話,[36] who said that an accomplished poet must be able to "depict a scene that is difficult to describe in such a way that it seems to be right before the eyes of the reader," thus helping to inspire a certain realism characteristic of Sung poetry and also identified by Lo and Schultz as a trait of Ch'ing poetry, which demonstrates, according to them, a "rise of realism."[37] It is hard to miss the tone of the crusader in Wu Chih-chen's poem, and he succeeded in helping direct the attention of many Ch'ing poets to the achievements of their Sung-dynasty forebears.

The poem to Sung Wan appears in Wu Chih-chen's collection only a few pages before a poem on New Year's eve for the year *hsin-hai* 辛亥,[38] corresponding for the most part to 1671, the year in which Wu Li was in the capital associating with Sung Wan and other members of the circle. Another of those members, Wang Mou-lin—the man for whom Wu Li apparently painted *My Hut Among Tall Bamboo* as described by Wang Shih-chen in a poem he probably inscribed on that painting and which has already been translated and discussed—himself has a poem entitled "Answering Wu Meng-chü," dating from 1671.[39] Wu Meng-chü is Wu Chih-chen; in a note to a line which tells us that Wu Chih-chen has been "studying Sung poetry," Wang Mou-lin writes: "Meng-chü at that time showed me his *Sung-shih ch'ao*." Would this have been the printed version—the book was printed sometime in 1671—or still the manuscript? In either case, we have Wu Chih-chen showing his important anthology to members of the Wang Shih-chen circle in the capital at the very time that Wu Li was associating with that circle. Although there is no proof, it seems likely that Wu Li too would have read the anthology and participated in the general rediscovery of Sung poetry. A Sung tonality is in fact pervasive in many of Wu Li's earlier, conventional poems, while the openness of Sung poetics to realistic description of new subject matter may have facilitated Wu's conception of the important series of thirty poems he was to write in the 1680s on life in Macao, filled with unprecedented details of Portuguese customs, to say nothing of the entire project of creating a Chinese Christian poetry.

The circle of poets gathered around Wang Shih-chen into which Wu Li was introduced had another, quite different interest in *tz'u* 詞 and *ch'ü* 曲 poetry, and indeed in drama and popular culture in general. We have seen that the author of one of the prefaces to MCSC, Yü Huai, also had an abiding interest in these matters. Lo and Schultz in fact speak of a full-fledged revival of *tz'u* poetry starting in the early Ch'ing.[40] Something of the enthusiasm for drama that prevailed in the Wang Shih-chen circle is conveyed by the title of a poem by Wang Mou-lin dating from 1672: "Surveillance Commissioner Yü-shu Invited Me to Accompany These Gentlemen—Minister of Revenue Liang, Vice-Minister of the Court of Imperial Sacrifices Kung, Hsi-ch'iao, and Yüan-t'ing—in Gathering at the Lodging Garden, Riding Out in Boats, Viewing Plays All Night Until Dawn, and Writing Poems."[41] The guests at this gala event included some of the most distinguished figures in the circle: Liang Ch'ing-piao 梁清標 (1620–1691), Kung Ting-tzu 龔鼎孳 (1615–1673), Wang Shih-lu 王士祿 (1626–1673)—the elder brother of Wang Shih-chen—and Wang Shih-chen himself. Two at least of these men (Liang and Kung) also knew Wu Li's closest friend, Hsü Chih-chien,[42] and it is tempting to imagine Wu himself included in similar gatherings.

Plays based on Confucian and historical themes seem to have been particularly moving to these men. Liang Ch'ing-piao has a poem about "Listening in the Rain to Pear Garden Musicians Performing the *ch'uan-ch'i* Play of Filial Son Huang,"[43] in which he conveys the heightened emotion of such an experience: "The grief and lamentation in this play [*ch'ü* 曲]—how very great! / On all four sides the audience hears, their tears profusely flow." Wu Li may already have encountered the idea that *ch'ü* could be used to convey serious subject matter while he was studying Confucianism with Ch'en Hu. Ch'en in a remarkable poem of his own praises the singing of a certain Ch'in Hsiao 秦簫, who performed three plays, or arias from them (also known as *ch'ü*), for a gathering of which he was part.[44] He writes that the singing "drew forth ten thousand kinds of sad feeling from me, / gave birth to gray hair on my head in a single evening; / tears too for this came to fall, / my heart too for this came to tremble." Ch'en was moved, in fact, to express a wish to write *ch'ü* about "righteous scholars and loyal ministers" for Ch'in Hsiao to sing, as he informs us in this same poem, in accordance with a general interest among certain Confucian scholars of the period in using popular culture to convey Confucian values—the same interest that gave rise to the so-called *shan-shu*

善書, or "morality books."[45] In such an environment, it is less sur-prising than at first encounter to discover that Wu Li would later choose the *san-ch'ü* 散曲 ("separate aria") form to write his most ambitious and experimental religious poems.

Ch'en Hu's desire to write *ch'ü* about "righteous scholars and loyal ministers" was in fact realized by his contemporary, Kuei Chuang 歸莊 (1613–1673), the great-grandson of the Ming prose writer Kuei Yu-kuang 歸有光 (1506–1571). Kuei Chuang com-posed a lengthy sequence of *ch'ü* called *Wan-ku ch'ou* 萬古愁 ("Sor-row of Ten Thousand Ages"),[46] beginning with the creation out of primal chaos by P'an-ku 盤古 and sweeping over the whole of Chinese history to culminate in the fall of Nanking in 1645. In a colophon to the work,[47] Ch'üan Tsu-wang 全祖望 (1705–1755) cites an observation by Shen Ch'üan 沈荃 (1624–1684) that the Shun-chih emperor (r. 1644–1661) so admired this piece that he had his court musicians set it to music and sing it during meals—a Chinese parallel, perhaps, to the Sinfonies pour les soupers du Roi soon to be composed for Louis XIV by Michel-Richard de Lalande (1657–1726), although these were purely instrumental. The success of this work in promulgating a Ming-loyalist perspec-tive on history within the very court may have impressed Wu Li and helped to prepare his decision to use the *ch'ü* for a very dif-ferent but at least equally weighty purpose.

In sum, Wu Li would have absorbed from his contact with Ch'ien Ch'ien-i, Ch'en Hu, and the Wang Shih-chen circle a broadly Sung-oriented taste in *shih* poetry, emphasizing realism with an openness to new subject matter and understated, relatively straightforward diction. At the same time he would have become interested in *tz'u* and *ch'ü* poetry, as well as drama, and would have developed a sensitivity to the possibilities of adopting these forms for serious uses.

# 2

# *Wu Li's Intellectual and Religious World*

To understand how Wu Li came to write his religious poetry, it is necessary to consider his intellectual and religious formation, especially while a student of Confucianism under Ch'en Hu. It is not impossible that Wu also gained some knowledge on the subject of religion while studying poetry with Ch'ien Ch'ien-i; Frederic Wakeman has recently described Ch'ien as "the first Chinese student of Tang Nestorianism, Manicheism and Mohammedanism,"[48] basing his statement on the account by L. Carrington Goodrich[49] of Ch'ien's essay *Ching-chiao k'ao* 景教考.[50] The Nestorian monument of 781 was discovered near Hsi-an sometime around 1624; Ch'ien, who would have heard of the discovery while in the capital, discusses at length in his essay various Western (Persian) religions, including Manicheism and Zoroastrianism, but reaches the erroneous conclusion that Nestorianism was simply the same as these last two. By the time Wu Li was studying with him, of course, Ch'ien may no longer have found the whole issue to have been of much interest.

Even a brief involvement, however, with the circle of Ch'en Hu, Lu Shih-i 陸世儀 (1611–1672), and their associates and followers must have exposed Wu Li to an atmosphere of intensive intellectual and spiritual ferment. Wakeman charactizes Lu Shih-i as a man "who reiterated the Cheng-Zhu ideal of 'dwelling in seriousness and investigating principles to the utmost' [*chü ching ch'iung li* 居敬窮理]," and thus part of a general revival of "Cheng-Zhu Confucianism" in the early Ch'ing, when scholars were seeking "an antidote...to moral relativism" and finding it in a call "to restore the absolute obligation of duties such as filial piety and loyalty."[51] This characterization is generally true of both Lu Shih-i and his close friend and colleague Ch'en Hu, but it fails to convey the intensity and depth of the intellectual questioning that was clearly progressing within this group of teachers and disciples.

Ch'en Hu and Lu Shih-i were indeed concerned with moral degeneration in their day and sought to reverse the decline by reinforcing traditional Confucian values while on the local level reestablishing the "village covenant" system—called for as well by the covert Catholic convert and anti-Buddhist polemicist (and poet) Wei I-chieh 魏裔介 (1616–1686)—and like him they wished to see what Wakeman terms "a restoration of the rites—a normative revolution."[52] These men had in view the creation of actual *hui* 會, "associations" formed for various purposes, including philanthropic. Jacques Gernet too has called attention to their importance and noted their similarity to Christian philanthropic groups; he specifically mentions one founded by Lu Shih-i in 1641.[53] Lu himself records that Ch'en Hu in turn founded four such *hui* at Wei village 蔚村, further dividing each *hui* into four smaller groups: a "lecture" association for talks to colleagues (*t'ung-chih* 同志) on the *I ching* 易經; a "repentance" (*ch'an* 懺) association to "bring together [*ho* 合] those in Wei village who serve Buddha"; a "local covenant [*hsiang-yüeh* 鄉約] to bring harmony to the village multitude"; and a "lotus society to join together friends in poetry and literature."[54] Lu also notes that on a day corresponding to January 27, 1649, two disciples of his were present who "did not like Buddha." Ch'en Hu, afraid they were deluded, wrote a poem to resolve their difficulty, including the line "Don't be surprised if the master [*hsien-sheng* 先生] is also Ch'an!" As we shall see, Ch'en Hu was to change his mind about the compatibility of Buddhism and Confucianism and in fact already had doubts about the issue at this time.

Ch'en Hu, Lu Shih-i, and their disciples were concerned not only with the revitalization of morality, but with specifically philosophical questions as well. A volume of their dialogues called *Huai-yün wen-ta* 淮雲問答 ("Questions and Answers Among the Clouds of the River Huai") records the responses of Ch'en, Lu, and others to questions of basic ontology and cosmology such as this one: "It

was asked: The ten thousand things are rooted in the Supreme
Ultimate. But where is the Supreme Ultimate?"[55] Ch'en's answer
is missing, but Lu Shih-i responded, "The Supreme Ultimate
appears disseminated among the ten thousand things," to which
Ch'en added the comment, "How bold and direct! Otherwise, one
would almost have to take the Supreme Ultimate to be a single
thing."

In another question, the problem of the relationship between
*t'ien* 天, "heaven," and *shang ti* 上帝, the "Lord on High," is
broached. Chu Hsi 朱熹 (1130–1200) himself, also in the question-
and-answer format, had taken up this matter when a disciple, cit-
ing various passages in the classics that refer to heaven as if it were
a being possessed of consciousness and will, asked: "In passages
like these, does it mean that there is really a master doing all this
up in the blue sky or does it mean that heaven has no personal
consciousness and the passages are merely deductions from
principle?"[56] Chu Hsi's response was that "these passages have the
same meaning. It is simply that principle [*li* 理] operates this
way." Ch'en Hu's questioner couches the problem in this fashion:
"The Duke of Chou took Hou Chi [Lord Millet] to be the equal of
heaven, and King Wen to be the equal of the Lord on High. Why
did he distinguish between heaven and the Lord on High in honor-
ing them [Hou Chi and King Wen]?"[57] In other words, if heaven
and the Lord on High are merely terms of reference to principle,
as Chu Hsi held them to be, why did the Duke of Chou distinguish
between them? Ch'en Hu answers as a true disciple of Chu Hsi:
"'Lord' [*ti* 帝] is precisely heaven. It is not that beyond heaven
there exists a so-called 'Lord.' The ten thousand things are rooted
in heaven."

But even the relationship of this heaven to phenomena is itself
questioned by one disciple, who poses this problem:[58]

> The *Chung-yung* 中庸 [Doctrine of the Mean] says, "The sun,
> moon, stars, and constellations are attached [*hsi* 繫] to it."[59]
> What things are the sun, moon, stars, and constellations? Do
> they possess substance [*chih* 質]? Do they lack substance? Is it
> that the four are attached to heaven? Or that heaven is
> attached to the four? How does the sun beam on people with
> light? How does the moon wax and wane? And how do the
> sun and moon perpetually pass through heaven? How do

stars fall? Why do the constellations have no fixed abode? Can it be that the methods of attachment of these various phenomena are dissimilar?

Ch'en Hu's answer is even more surprising than the question:

> Matters pertaining to heaven we cannot seek out. We speak of matters pertaining to man and no more. If we must speak of matters pertaining to heaven, then we cannot but depend on books, and yet if we base ourselves on the explanations in books, I am afraid they will prove inadequate to make us believe in them, and indeed they will cause us to doubt. As for the sun, moon, stars, and constellations, they consist of material energy [*ch'i* 氣]. That they are without substance is firmly established.

If Wu Li participated in discussions such as these—and he must have done so—his searching mind must have been impressed by Ch'en's willingness to acknowledge the inadequacy of explanations for certain phenomena in the Chinese classics. Such acknowledgment may have helped prepare him to accept the apparently greater knowledge of such matters brought to China by the Jesuits. More important, Ch'en Hu's discussion of the seemingly personal *shang ti* of the classics as merely a form of reference to the impersonal *li* may have been unconvincing to Wu, and thus increased the likelihood that once exposed to the Jesuits' claim that the *shang ti* of the classics was in fact none other than the supreme God of the Bible, and that the Neo-Confucian equation of *shang ti* with *li* was actually a betrayal of an earlier knowledge of God, Wu Li might well have been disposed to agree. That the question could be raised at all implies a certain unease with the whole issue on the part of at least some individuals—an unease which, for that matter, must have existed as early as the twelfth century when a similar question was raised in the circle of Chu Hsi. Given such an intellectual environment, the readiness of a man like Wu Li to embrace such a seemingly alien creed as Catholicism becomes slightly less puzzling.

The degree of questioning that flourished in the Ch'en Hu circle is nowhere more apparent than in a truly extraordinary poem by

one of Ch'en's chief disciples, a certain Ch'ü Yu-chung 瞿有仲.
The poem is collected in the *Ts'ung-yu chi* 從游集, a book dating to
1659 in which, as Ch'ien Ch'ien-i relates in a preface he wrote for
it,[60] Ch'en Hu "critiques and arranges the poems of his disciples."
Ch'en Yüan long ago noted that no poems of Wu Li are to be
found in current editions of this book, attributing this surprising
hiatus to the apparent brevity of Wu Li's sojourn as a student of
Ch'en Hu, but also noting that the two men exchanged poems
during a trip they undertook together in 1664, poems which were
then gathered in a separate volume also called *Ts'ung-yu chi*![61]
(This second book apparently no longer exists, but some at least
of the poems exchanged by Wu and Ch'en are to be found in their
respective collections.)[62]

The poem by Ch'ü Yu-chung, entitled *Chün t'ien yüeh* 鈞天樂,
"Music of Harmonious Heaven,"[63] is important for several reasons
and is therefore translated here in full:

> Music of Harmonious Heaven
> When Azure Heaven had temporarily died,
>> Yellow Heaven was born;
> he held a high banquet at Jasper Terrace
>> to entertain the hundred gods.
> Heaven's drums sounded—boom, boom—
>> the Heavenly Music played in welcome;
> before half the wine was served,
>> they summoned the Jade Fairies:
> when their Rainbow Robe ballet was done,
>> they all played on reed organs.
> I suddenly bestrode a cloud,
>> my feet trod on the stars;
> I somersaulted with a leap and entered the empyrean.
> This humble subject with ceremonious step
>> prostrated himself within the pepper courtyard;
> His Majesty looked at me without recognition
>> and said, "What man is this?"
> Hands in reverential posture, I kowtowed,
>> and spoke with full sincerity:

"This subject has certain doubts
    and wishes to submit them on high.

"I dare not infringe upon taboos
    by discussing contemporary affairs;

"rather let me speak of one or two matters
    from the days of Fu Hsi and Shen Nung.

"Your Majesty, be so kind as to give me your attention.

"Heaven obtained unity and was perpetually pure;

"Earth obtained purity and was perpetually tranquil.

"Man obtained the material energy of heaven and earth
    and took on form;

"and since his form was taken on,

"what has happened during the next mere
    three million two hundred sixty-nine thousand and
    eighty-two years?

"There was the confusion of emperors and lords,
    of the Yin dynasty and the Hsia, of the Chou, and of the
    Ch'in!

"Just because P'an-ku transformed his one body,

"his eyes became the sun and moon, his breath the clouds,

"his blood and fluids the rivers and lakes, his voice the thunder,

"his sinews and flesh the fields and earth, his hairs the constellations;

"then in massive heat, when wind swept up the dust,

"it scattered and flew in all six directions
    and became the black-haired people.

"Then Nü-wa was still more officious:

"she smelted rocks to patch the western vault.

"But still she thought that people were too few,

"so she molded earth and strung rope.

"At that time material energy and images
    were still imbued with purity—

"but Ts'ang Chieh for no reason
    created written characters!

"Primal chaos suddenly divided, heaven and earth
    were startled;

"every night was heard the sobbing of the dragon mother!

"And thus was it caused that for a thousand ages
      men would suffer the carving of their hearts and spitting out
      of blood,
"the cutting of their livers and slicing of their kidneys
"to help fill up the pit of the Ancestral Dragon!
"Can withered grasses serve as omen?
"Can the dead tortoise be vitalized again?
"Fu Hsi proceeded to diagram heaven and plan out earth,
"to outline Yin and divide the Yang,
"thus carving out the scheming mind from primal chaos.
"The scheming mind formed the pit where histories were burned;
"how could the Dark Lady help but speak of weapons?
"In wind and cloud, serpents and birds
      daily grew more chaotic:
"how could the White Emperor not construct the wall?
"Constructing misery, constructing sorrow,
      with swarming wails of grief!
"If they were not attacking, they were defending,
"if not campaigning, then invading:
"fathers lamenting for their sons,
"mothers forced to cast off children.
"From afar they gazed towards Yen-jan Mountain
"where, stacked up like so many rocks,
"white bones were piled into tumuli.
"Heaven resides in the highest place,
      with heart of great humaneness:
"seeing this, how could it not feel compassion and pain?
"This subject has something to say, exalted and serene;
"this subject has a plan, wondrous, comprehensive:
"Why not establish a single lord for all of heaven and earth?
"Why not establish a single people for all of heaven and earth?
"Man would never be born and never die;
"nations would never perish and never arise.
"The jade toad would never wane;
"the *jo-mu* tree would seasonably shine.

"The sun would forget to rise and sink, eliminating midnight;

"the frost and snow would be withdrawn,
    it would always be like spring.

"The people would be illiterate and clodlike,
    complete in innocence;

"they would know nothing of weapons; harmoniously
    they would preserve their bodies whole.

"They would take peaceful pleasure in uncivilized wilderness,

"enjoying the greenery of plants and trees.

"Would not human society then stop its hustle and bustle?

"And heaven too with such an arrangement
    would be spared its constant change.

"The ice peach would no longer bloom only to fade;

"the P'eng-lai isles of the immortals
    would never be far away.

"How would anyone even dream
    of bestowing the barbarian dog upon Chao?

"How would the Quail's Head territory
    ever be wrongly bestowed upon Ch'in?"

Even before this subject's words were done, the Lord
    showed signs of inattention:

with a smile, he looked left and right
    where they plucked the sonorous zithers.

The zithers sounded—thrum, thrum—the singing was rich and
    full;

whale bells and tiger flutes rang out loud and clear.

This subject wished to speak again—but he seemed not to hear;

I kowtowed, urgently knocking my head against the steps
    until my blood did flow.

The Lord then said, "My son, please desist from struggle:

"this matter is out of the ordinary; we simply cannot do it.

"We will for the nonce exhaust our daily pleasure;

"when Azure Heaven is born again,
    he will carry this out for you."

The title of this ambitious poem alludes to music performed in
the "innermost of the nine divisions of heaven" (A. C. Graham)[64]

and heard by King (or Duke) Mu of Chou (or Ch'in) when a magician from the far West took him on a magical dream journey to this wonderful place, as narrated in *Lieh Tzu* 列子 and alluded to by Chang Heng 張衡 (78–139) in his *Prosepoem on the Western Capital* 西京賦.[65] In *Lieh Tzu* (as translated by Graham), "the King really believed that he was enjoying 'the mighty music of the innermost heaven' [*chün t'ien ta-yüeh* 鈞天大樂], in the Pure City or the Purple Star, the palaces where God [*ti* 帝] dwells."[66] Chang Heng writes (in the translation of David R. Knechtges): "Anciently, the Great Lord of Heaven was pleased with Duke Mu of Qin, invited him to court, and feted him with the 'Grand Music of Harmonious Heaven' [*chün t'ien kuang-yüeh* 鈞天廣樂]."[67]

The episode in *Lieh Tzu* of a mystical or dream journey to heaven where the Grand Music is to be heard seems to have impressed not only Ch'ü Yu-chung, but Wu Li as well. In the fifth of his important series of nine poems entitled "Moved to Sing of the Truth of Holy Church" (*kan yung sheng-hui chen-li* 感咏聖會真理),[68] Wu Li will borrow the phrase *chün t'ien kuang-yüeh* (although reversing the two elements: *kuang-yüeh chün t'ien*) as a description of the music of Heaven. The poem as a whole attempts to conjure up the paradisiacal atmosphere of the Christian Heaven by the use of phrases that derive for the most part from classical Confucian and Taoist texts:

> The Grand Music in Harmonious Heaven plays;
> in joyful leaping, there gather all the saints!
> Instruments blowing, the gold trumpet sounds;
> tones harmonizing, phoenix and lion conduct.
> This "inner scene" has limitless light;
> the True Flower is endlessly fragrant.
> In this place a single day
> is a thousand years in the ordinary world.

But if Wu Li will use a traditional phrase to help depict the Heaven of his faith, for Ch'ü Yu-chung the title of his poem takes on an element of irony. For in this poem, as Ch'en Hu exclaims in a note at the end, "a whole bellyful of stifled grief is expressed," and if anything, to borrow a phrase from C. S. Lewis, God—or at least one of the five emperors of the five directions—is here placed in the dock. Ch'ü implies that Yellow Heaven has usurped his position from Azure Heaven. In the histories, "Yellow Heaven" is often associated with the late-Han rebel Chang Chüeh 張角. The connection was so well established that even the popular novel *San-kuo chih yen-i* 三國志演義, borrowing a phrase from the biography of Huang-fu Sung 皇甫嵩 in the *Hou Han shu* 後漢書, has Chang Chüeh promulgating the idea that "Azure Heaven has already died; Yellow Heaven must be established" (*Ts'ang t'ien i ssu, huang t'ien tang li* 蒼天已死, 黃天當立).[69] But Ch'ü Yu-chung's implication throughout his poem is that Yellow Heaven has actually presided—irresponsibly—over the whole of history, starting from the very creation by P'an-ku and Nü-wa, and that the entirety of history has consisted of disharmony and suffering. (One is reminded of the Gnostic heresy according to which the Creation was actually the work of an evil demiurge.) The poet therefore travels to heaven and prostrates himself before Yellow Heaven (and despite Ch'en Hu's and Chu Hsi's view that "heaven" is simply a term for "principle," Yellow Heaven is depicted as a person). His reception is icy: "What man is this?" is all that Yellow Heaven has to say in greeting.

The poet proceeds to lay before Yellow Heaven his "doubts" (*i* 疑—the same word used by Ch'en Hu in the dialogue about the mode of attachment of the heavenly bodies to heaven itself): "[The explanations for these bodies in the classics] will prove inadequate to make us believe in them, and indeed they will cause us to doubt [*shih jen i yeh* 使人疑也]." Perhaps disingenuously, the poet declines to discuss "contemporary affairs" and proceeds instead to "speak of one or two matters from the days of Fu Hsi and Shen Nung," but these turn out to entail virtually the whole of early history from the creation through the Ch'in dynasty. Surprisingly, instead of the Confucian view that a golden age under the early sage-emperors gave way to eras of progressive decadence, an essentially Taoist perspective is presented, familiar from the *Tao te ching* 道德經 (and again reminiscent of Gnosticism), to the effect that a primordial unity was tragically disrupted by the very act of creation—P'an-ku's body becoming the universe, and human beings evolving from the dust swept up by a primeval wind, or formed from earth and rope by Nü-wa. (Both accounts are given with no attempt to reconcile them.) The creation of written characters by Ts'ang Chieh 倉頡,[70] instead of being seen as a major step toward civilization, is castigated as a meaningless act, a fall from the original undifferentiated purity. The succession of dynasties is presented as mere confusion, causing nothing but untold suffering to those caught in the web of "defending, campaigning, invading"; "fathers lamenting for their sons, / mothers forced to cast off children." Ch'ü may not refer specifically to more recent events in China—the fall of the Ming—but they haunt his poem if only because of the very intensity of the feelings he expresses, but also in accordance with the long-established rhetorical technique of using events of the past to *allude* to events of the present.

The poet now presents a scheme of his own to rectify the abysmal situation. He proposes the establishment of a *single lord* for all heaven and earth (as opposed to the system of five "heavens"), and that of a "single people" (that is, a unified population no longer fragmented by dynastic or other loyalties), and beyond that a Taoist utopia inspired again by the *Tao te ching*. "The people would be illiterate and clodlike" and therefore "complete in innocence." "They would know nothing of weapons," and would live in perfect harmony with nature. And heaven would return to a state of permanent harmony; time itself would stop. (The combination of revulsion at nearly the whole of history and civilization itself with utopian yearnings for a return to primal harmony with nature is strikingly reminiscent of the Enlightenment position taking form in Europe at the same time.) But Ch'ü's plan is met with indifference by Yellow Heaven. He continues to listen to the "Music of Harmonious Heaven"—here clearly representing sybaritic indulgence rather than the celestial joy it will come to evoke in Wu Li's poem—callously indifferent to the urging of the poet's plea. Even when the poet draws his own blood by knocking his head against the steps of the throne, Yellow Heaven openly announces his intention of continuing to indulge in pleasure until such time as "Azure Heaven is born again" (and will presumably assume responsibility for the disastrous situation willfully ignored by Yellow Heaven). The central question of the poem is asked at lines 55 and

56: "Heaven resides in the highest place, with heart of greatest humaneness: / seeing this, how could it not feel compassion and pain?"

Although the poem raises the question of whether heaven possesses feeling and consciousness, and adopts an almost completely Taoist view of history, the Neo-Confucian Ch'en Hu approves of it and gives it pride of place as the first poem by Ch'ü Yu-chung in the section devoted to his work in *Ts'ung-yu chi*. Perhaps he senses that the poem is not really intended to be philosophically or theologically serious—that Ch'ü may not be committed to the doctrines implied by the poem but is rather employing a type of hyperbole to convey his "stifled grief." Still, one cannot help but marvel that Ch'ü's sense of dissatisfaction is here carried to the very doorstep of heaven; such a poem must have emerged from an environment of intense questioning.

It has already been suggested that Kuei Chuang's *Wan-ku ch'ou* may have contributed to Wu Li's idea of using the *san-ch'ü* genre for serious subject matter. Ch'ü Yu-chung's poem is a *shih*, perhaps best seen as belonging to the *Yüeh-fu* 樂府 ("Music Bureau" ballad) tradition, but it is certainly possible that in his case, the Kuei Chuang poem may have suggested the adoption of a questioning or even sarcastic attitude toward the whole sweep of history. Kuei too begins with the creation from primal chaos, referring at the very outset to P'an-ku,[71] and he ridicules the sage-emperor Yao and other Confucian culture heroes for various errors they supposedly committed, using the expression *"hsiao, hsiao, hsiao"* 笑笑笑: "laughable, laughable, laughable!" Kuei, as we have seen (see note 46), wrote a eulogy on a portrait of Ch'ien Ku (Mei-hsien),[72] who according to Ch'en Hu was Ch'ü Yu-chung's closest friend and the author of the preface to Ch'ü's (apparently lost) poetry collection.[73] Kuei certainly knew other members of the Ch'ü clan from Ch'ü Yu-chung's hometown of Ch'ang-shu 常熟, including Ch'ü Shih-ssu 瞿式耜 (1590–1651),[74] himself like Wu Li both a disciple of Ch'ien Ch'ien-i and a convert to Catholicism; Ch'ü was baptized by Fr. Giulio Aleni, S.J. (1582–1649). (The Ch'ü clan in fact produced a number of converts, as pointed out by J. C. Yang and T. Numata.)[75] Of course, it is also possible that such an attitude was "in the air" among those sympathetic to the Ming cause and that Ch'ü Yu-chung was not directly or even indirectly influenced by the Kuei Chuang poem.

Given the atmosphere of dissatisfaction and questioning that clearly prevailed in the Ch'en Hu circle, and is reflected in the poetry written by such a disciple of Ch'en's as Ch'ü Yu-chung, it is not surprising to find, also reflected in the poetry of the circle, frequent reference to acts of conversion from Confucianism to Buddhism and, in one case, from Taoism to Buddhism. As our ultimate concern will be to examine the influence of Wu Li's conversion on his poetry, let us concentrate on reflections of conversion activity in the poetry of the Ch'en Hu circle, and then attempt to gauge the attitude of Ch'en Hu and his associates toward the religion to which most of the converts seem to have been attracted: Buddhism.

We begin with the unique case of a certain Yüan Yu-pai 袁幼白, whose strange pilgrimage is briefly recounted in the title of a group of four *chüeh-chü* quatrains by Lu Shih-i:

> Master Yüan Yu-pai is an old classmate of mine. He can write literature, is fond of knight-errantry, and is good at chanting [poetry] and whistling. Formerly he studied to become an immortal [*hsüeh hsien* 學仙], but now, suddenly, he goes off to devote himself to studying the Wheel of the Law. About to leave, he has requested poems as parting gifts, and I have playfully formed four quatrains to take the place of *gāthā* [*chieh* 偈].[76]

The poems themselves are indeed playful in tone, full of the paradoxical—and sometimes impenetrable—humor so characteristic of Ch'an Buddhist poetry. The first two are given here in tentative translation:

1

As a youth you leapt wildly, older, do Ch'an meditation:
cut in half as two people, you were just hanging there!
How is it that from the first
    there *is* no second teaching?
You turn a somersault and fly right to blue heaven!

2

When flourishing flowers have all faded,
  you'll be enlightened to the King of Void!
After enlightenment, there's nothing to keep you
  from flourishing flowers again.
This man of letters of the "enterprise of wisdom"
  was studying the Way;
grinding bricks to make a mirror—might as well
  wet your bed!

These poems would certainly seem to take a (Ch'an) Buddhist viewpoint, from the use of technical terms such as *wu erh* 無二— "There is no second [vehicle to enlightenment]"—from the second chapter of the *Lotus Sutra*[77] to the well-known koan in which "grinding bricks to make a mirror" represents useless effort toward enlightenment. For Lu Shih-i, as a Confucian, such as attitude can only have been adopted in a "playful" manner, as he himself tells us it was in his title. Still, even here a serious point is broached when the issue is raised in the first poem of whether there is a "second teaching." Taoism and Buddhism were often thought to go together, especially by their opponents—for example, Han Yü 韓愈 (768–824)—but also at times by admirers like the poet P'an Lei 潘耒 (1646–1708), who describes a visit to the Temple of the Reclining Buddha in a poem written sometime before 1672,[78] and ends inspired by his surroundings to announce that "if the Valley Spirit can be sought, / I will nurture the Mysterious Female." The well-known terms from the *Tao te ching* seem to P'an entirely consistent with his Buddhist environment. But Lu Shih-i's classmate Yüan Yu-pai did apparently feel compelled to break with one and adhere to the other.

More common by far were conversions from Confucianism to Buddhism. Ch'en Hu reacted to these, it would appear, more in sadness than in anger. In the title to a poem,[79] he relates that "Yüan Shih-min 袁石民 resigned from his local school as a well-known *chu-sheng* 諸生 degree-holder and lived in retirement in a village to the north for over twenty years. Now he has cast off his home to become a monk. Lamenting his decision, I have sent him a poem." Ch'en does not set out to chastise the man, but rather to express his sadness—he "laments" (*ai* 哀) the decision—and even ends, perhaps with a touch of irony, "With your rounded pate [tonsured head] and square monk's robe you repair unto the realm of purity, / laughing at me for staying to the end of my years on this muddy, weedy turf." This may be Ch'en's gentle way of telling the man not to expect Ch'en to follow in his footsteps. Would Ch'en's reaction to the news of Wu Li's conversion have been similar?

Still more telling for our understanding of Ch'en Hu's attitude toward conversions to Buddhism is a preface he wrote "To See Off the Monk Erh-sheng on His Journey to Wu-i Mountain."[80] The preface recounts how this man was Ch'en's

> friend from beyond this realm. Moved deeply by the changes in the world [a reference to the Ming-Ch'ing transition], he burned his Confucian scholar's cap and escaped into Buddhism. It has been a long time now since he freely found his way, rejecting external phenomena. Only an obsession [*p'i* 癖] with mountains and bodies of water has he not been able to cast away from his heart. . . . So he placed himself upon the thirty-six peaks [of the Yellow Mountains in Anhui province], and wherever he went, he would inevitably write poems, and for each poem there would inevitably be a travel account. If he had encountered a halcyon age, he could certainly have trod the kingly path [served in government] with energy to spare. But now, unfortunately, he has become a disciple of Buddha, running, climbing, and fording his way among mountaintops and watery banks, thus expanding his spirit and wasting his months and years. Could it be that he has dissatisfaction [*pu tzu tsu* 不自足] within? I love the forcefulness of his will, but regret his not meeting with the right times.

There is no doubt that Ch'en considers Erh-sheng's choice to be unfortunate, but he is nevertheless highly empathetic, blaming the badness of the times rather than Erh-sheng himself for having made a poor decision, and in fact expressing admiration for the depth of Erh-sheng's feelings about the traumatic "changes in the world."

Clearly the attitude toward Buddhism (and therefore toward conversions to it) which prevailed in the Ch'en Hu circle was ambivalent. It will be recalled that at one point, Ch'en Hu had gently chided two disciples of Lu Shih-i for their antipathy to Buddhism. But in a document dating from the third month of the crucial year of 1644, entitled "Proclamation of a Covenant to Drive Away All Monks" 約都逐僧徒檄 and apparently surviving only in the form of a Ch'ing-dynasty manuscript in the Library of Congress,[81] Ch'en complains that "since this spring began, Buddhism has burgeoned throughout the nation 'like crazy' [*ju k'uang* 如狂]; I am quite indignant about it, and so have written this proclamation." Ch'en here declares Buddhism to be more poisonous in effect than robbers and bandits, "actors and dwarfs." Less vehemently, in a preface addressed to another of the Buddhist monks with whom he did maintain friendships, on the occasion of seeing the monk off to take his vows,[82] Ch'en actually praises Buddhism for holding to the various prohibitions (*chieh* 戒), which make possible at least coexistence without harm to Confucianism, while pointing out that "Buddhism casts aside human relationships, and bases its doctrine on the void and extinction." He notes that some may consider Confucianism to be too strict, but that Buddhism "is especially difficult to practice, given human feelings."

The subject of the relationship between Confucianism and Buddhism, as might be expected, arose during the philosophical discussions that took place among Ch'en Hu, his associates like Lu Shih-i and others, and his disciples. On one occasion, someone raised this question:

> Our Confucian way combines essence and function [*t'i-yung* 體用], hence it is very far removed from the emptiness of the Buddhists. . . . [Here he calls attention to the necessity for abstention and effort in Confucianism.] . . . How does this differ from the painstaking cultivation of the Buddhists?[83]

The speaker also asks about certain other possible points of similarity between the two. Ch'en Hu's detailed answer to this question is lost, but the reply of Sheng Ching 盛敬 (*tzu*, Sheng-ch'uan 聖傳) is preserved and probably conveys Ch'en's perspective. Sheng, together with Ch'en, Lu Shih-i, and a certain Chiang Shih-shao 江士韶, was one of a grouping of four thinkers known as "Lu,

Ch'en, Sheng, and Chiang."[84] Like Ch'en in his preface to the
monk about to take vows, Sheng says: "The painstaking effort of
the Buddhists may be similar to the hard work undertaken by us
Confucians, but the reason we do not emulate them is that the
Buddhists' effort is in search of the void . . . while the effort of us
Confucians is in search of something substantial [*shih* 實]." Sheng
further criticizes the Ch'eng brothers and Chu Hsi for the youthful
error of interest in Buddhism, which they themselves corrected
upon hearing of the "orthodox Way" (*cheng tao* 正道).

In sum, then, it would probably be accurate to say that Ch'en
Hu and his circle in general rejected what to them was the nihilis-
tic tendency of Buddhist doctrine, while admiring, somewhat
grudgingly, the abstemious rigor of the lives led by individual
Buddhist monks, maintaining friendships in fact with a number of
these latter, some of whom had indeed emerged from their own
ranks. Moreover, it was generally considered that these men had
"left the world" at a time when the world was well worth leaving.
It must also have been recognized that a certain proportion of
these "conversions," perhaps even the greater part, were more acts
of political protest than they were true religious conversions.

A final point to be made about the profuse conversion activity in
early Ch'ing China is that reconversions (to Buddhism and back
again) were not unheard of. The best-documented case is that of
the great scholar and poet Ch'ü Ta-chün 屈大均 (1630–1696),
whose "Discourse on Returning to Confucianism" 歸儒說 is a key
document for the study of the whole subject.[85] Concerned to de-
fend himself against any charge of betrayal of Confucianism that
might be leveled by those who were less understanding than Ch'en
Hu, Ch'ü opens as follows:

> When I was twenty-two, I studied Ch'an. After this, I also
> studied Mystery [*hsüan* 玄: Taoism]. Only when I reached the
> age of thirty did I realize my mistake, so I completely cast
> them off and once again devoted myself to our Confucianism.
> For our Confucianism is able to encompass the other two
> schools, while the two schools cannot encompass our Con-
> fucianism. If you have the two schools, you cannot do with-
> out our Confucianism, while if you have our Confucianism,
> you can do without the two schools.

Later in the essay he deplores a tendency to blur the distinctions between Confucianism and Ch'an Buddhism:

> Ch'an at this time is like our Confucianism in that neither can maintain its purity. Thus when Ch'an is compounded with Confucian elements, should a Ch'anist study it, he will lose that which makes Ch'an Ch'an. When Confucianism is compounded with Ch'an elements, should a Confucian study it, he will lose that which makes Confucianism Confucianism.

Thus does Ch'ü take his stand against the religious syncretism that had developed in the course of the Ming dynasty and continued to be a factor in the religious life of the early Ch'ing.

In general, then, it is apparent that both within the Ch'en Hu circle where Wu Li learned his Ch'eng-Chu brand of Neo-Confucianism, and more broadly among the literati in general in the first several decades of the new Ch'ing dynasty, not only was there unprecedented intellectual and spiritual turmoil, but there was a spate of conversions among the three teachings of China, especially from Confucianism to Buddhism. The great question, of course, is therefore not so much why Wu Li converted to something, as why he chose Christianity. The action is a puzzle from several points of view. Certainly it is conventional wisdom among scholars of the period to describe the later seventeenth century as a time of decline in literati conversions to Christianity. Gernet refers to a "déclin de l'influence chrétienne en Chine à partir du milieu du XVIIᵉ siècle."[86] Mungello puts it this way: "Changes in the intellectual climate in China [in the late seventeenth century] had made the literati less open to the sort of persuasion Ricci had built into his accommodation formula. With the death of literati converts of the stature of Li Chih-tsao 李之藻 (1565–1630) and Hsü Kuang-ch'i 徐光啟 (1562–1633) and with the *failure to convert new literati of like stature* after the ascent of the Manchus in 1644, the Jesuits were increasingly dependent upon imperial support" (emphasis added).[87] Was Wu Li simply a bizarre exception to the rule? (And what about the other two Chinese ordained along with him in 1688?)

By the same token, in his magnum opus on the Ming-Ch'ing

transition, Wakeman follows Benjamin Elman and Lynne A. Struve in identifying "a kind of secularism" in early Ch'ing thought,[88] and he follows W. J. Bouwsma in drawing a parallel with intellectual developments in seventeenth-century Europe. Was Wu Li the Blaise Pascal (1623–1662) of China, a lone representative of piety in an increasingly secular age? What is one to say of those far more numerous Buddhist converts who were not mere political protesters? Is it not possible that rather than a pervasive secularization, one is confronted both in Europe and in China with a parting of the ways, between secularists and pietists, with the former increasingly the dominant force in intellectual life and therefore in a position to relate intellectual history in a manner reflective of their own beliefs?

More subtly, Lin Xiaoping in a recent article attempts to present Wu Li's conversion as a rebellion "away from the constraints of the Confucian Five Relations toward a more genuine humanity."[89] He strives to establish that Wu Li read Aquinas's *Summa Theologica* in the Chinese translation of Ludovicus Buglio (1606–1682) on the basis of a single line of Wu's poetry, the second line from a couplet in the poem "Echoing a Friend's Poem, 'New Green'": *wu ch'ing ch'un hou hsien; / ch'ao hsing chü chung shen* 物情春後見, 超性句中深 .[90] Lin translates the line in question, "I read *Chaoxing xueyao* 超性學要 [Buglio's rendition of the title of the *Summa*], and found it profound." He then proceeds to argue that Wu was inspired by the Aristotelian aesthetics of Aquinas to pay closer attention to actual nature.[91] But the argument seems tenuous indeed; in the fuller context of the poem, the crucial line might simply be intended as praise for the original poem by Wu's friend: "(The feelings of things now with spring appear; / ) the transcendent nature in your lines is deep." Wu probably, of course, read parts at least of the *Summa* while in theological training in Macao (although the painting discussed by Lin dates from 1676 and Wu went to Macao in 1681), or he may have seen parts of Buglio's as yet not fully printed translation prior to that. Lu Lung-chi 陸隴其 (1630–1693), a scholar and diarist who contributed a poem in the archaic four-character meter to the collected writings of the *Sung-shih ch'ao* compiler, Wu Chih-chen,[92] records that in 1675 Buglio actually showed him the manuscript of his incompletely printed translation—so the work was in circulation at that time.[93] Lu Lung-chi himself, who also had the experience of meeting with another leading Jesuit, Ferdinand Verbiest (1623–1688), was sufficiently interested to record these events in his diary, and was generally impressed by Western learning, but two key doctrines of Christianity he felt compelled to reject: "That which cannot be believed in the teaching of the Westerners is in particular the doctrine of Adam and Eve and the theory of Jesus's Incarnation."[94]

Although Wu Li himself must have felt compelled to reject aspects of Neo-Confucianism, these would certainly not have included the Five Relations; he would have been more likely, as certain poems reveal, to have rejected points of ontology and cosmology, such as the account of evolutionary emergence of phenomena from a "Supreme Ultimate," which stood in flat contradiction to the account of the Creation by God in Genesis. And if Wu was inspired by anything in the *Summa* or other theological books, it would have been precisely the Christian doctrines expressed there. The Aristotelian elements would have been of secondary importance for him, as they were for Aquinas himself, particularly as Chinese aesthetic theory as early as the great literary theoreticians of the Six Dynasties period did encompass a kind of mimetic theory of artistic creativity in which the poet or artist goes directly to nature for inspiration.[95] This idea, by late Ming and early Ch'ing times, may have been observed more in the breach than in the observance, but the theory at least was reiterated by the Kung-an school and their followers and is implicit in the whole concept of "Sung poetry." Even if Wu responded in some way to the Aristotelian elements in Aquinas, the fact would still beg the question at issue: Why did he become a Christian?

In probably the most intelligent attempt yet made to probe the why and wherefore of Chinese conversions to Christianity, Willard J. Peterson, limiting himself to the study of the "three pillars of the Chinese church"—Yang T'ing-yün 楊廷筠 (1557–1627), Li Chih-tsao, and Hsü Kuang-ch'i—appropriately reminds us that "the minds and hearts of [these men] would not be fully accessible even if one could subject them to all sorts of prying interrogations. Available sources do not provide sufficient evidence to analyze any profound religious experience they may have undergone."[96] If these remarks are true of the three pillars, they are even truer of Wu Li in that we simply do not possess documents detailing the process of his conversion. Nevertheless, his religious poems and recorded sayings do serve as a source for some understanding of his theological interests and do hint, however distantly, at a "profound religious experience" beginning in intellectual, moral, and spiritual dissatisfaction and culminating in conversion.

Peterson's sensitive characterization of Yang T'ing-yün in particular may, in my view, be applied to Wu Li as well. Yang "was troubled about what he, and many of his concerned contemporaries, perceived as a pervasive moral decay." He "sought to identify what is 'right.' . . . The opportunity was present for him to find it in Neo-Confucianism. . . . He also sought it in Buddhist teachings, provided by the clerics to whom he gave contributions. They both failed him." He was "searching in effect for an externally determined source of moral values as an alternative to the relativism and introspection which prevailed among many of his contemporaries."[97]

That Wu Li saw matters in a similar light is implied by certain passages in his poems and recorded statements. Ch'en Yüan has called attention to a particularly significant couplet from the third in a group of "Seven Miscellaneous Poems—Following Rhymes" in Wu's *San-yü chi* 三餘集, a collection which remained in manuscript form until it was printed in 1937 and then annotated by Fang Hao in 1967.[98] In this poem, written in 1690 when Wu was fifty-nine years of age by Chinese reckoning, Wu begins by telling us, "Recently I have been studying the learning of Western characters," a reference, according to Fang Hao, to Wu's ongoing interest in mastering Latin. The third couplet of this regulated-verse poem reads, *hsin chien kuan ch'u wang*; / *chüeh wu na k'ou fei* 忻見官除妄; / 絕無衲叩扉: "I'm delighted to see an official extirpating error; / absolutely no monk's-robes knock at my gate." Both of these lines are important for determining Wu's intellectual and religious development. As Ch'en Yüan points out, the first is a reference to the campaign against "decadent shrines" (*yin tz'u* 淫祠) in the Suchou region conducted with great vigor by the provincial governor, T'ang Pin 湯斌 (1627–1687), a powerful official with enough of a reputation as a poet to be anthologized in *Ch'ing-shih pieh-ts'ai chi* and *Ch'ing-shih chi-shih*.[99] The edict which T'ang himself issued on the occasion of taking the original measures in 1685 is preserved in his collected writings and reads in part as follows:

> Whereas the Wu area traditionally has many decadent shrines, and Shang-fang Mountain is especially egregious— evil demons there having deceived people lo these several hundreds of years—men and women from far and near day and night rushing there so that the degenerate custom has by now reached an acute state, as soon as this official stepped down from his carriage he issued a prohibition barring these practices. The women who came to the place to offer incense lessened by comparison with before. But unexpectedly, this official had to go to the Huai region on famine relief, and the time happened to correspond with a festival, so men and women again gathered there. This official, reflecting that when the human heart has been deluded and confused for a long time it cannot be brought to enlightenment by a proclamation in mere words, took the clay images of the shrine and threw them in the waters of Great Lake, and took the wood-carved images and consigned them to flaming bonfires, so that they have all become mud or ashes. In addition, he considered that the place continuing to exist, after several years wicked religious masters and shamans would inevitably run amuck and perverted doctrines once again arise; only if an alternate image of a deity, staunch and strong, orthodox and straight, were to be erected, would it suffice to suppress the demons and bring awe to the people's hearts.[100]

T'ang goes on to describe how he had an imposing image of Kuan Yü—"His Holy Highness Lord Kuan" 關聖帝君—sculpted in clay and the proper ceremonies and sacrifices conducted. A modern anthropologist might see this as the suppression of popular folk-religious cults (of particular attractiveness, it would appear, to women) in favor of an officially sanctioned state cult, but we are more interested in the way T'ang himself and his contemporary literati saw the event. Among the important literati who praised T'ang Pin for his efforts were Lü Liu-liang, co-compiler of the *Sung-shih ch'ao,* Wang Shih-chen, Yu T'ung 尤侗 (1618–1704)—poet, dramatist, and scholar who wrote an important preface to Wu Li's *San-pa chi* 三巴集 as we shall see—and Lu Lung-chi, the diarist who met Jesuit missionaries and was impressed by them.[101] Lü Liu-liang, in his letter to a friend, expresses his admiration and even pleasant astonishment that this pernicious and hitherto intractable problem has apparently been dealt with once and for all. Wang Shih-chen actually claims credit for having persuaded T'ang Pin to act. In his collection of random notes, *Ch'ih-pei ou-t'an* 池北偶談,[102] Wang writes: "T'ang . . . stopped by my place of lodging, and I told him how the women of Wu loved to enter temples to burn incense, and that this must in the first instance be prohibited. T'ang agreed with me, forcefully carried out such measures in Wu, and customs underwent a change."

In fact, the proclamations issued by T'ang during his earlier tenure in Chianghsi indicate that he was already taking similar measures there.[103] In some of these, and in his Suchou documents, T'ang either quotes directly the relevant provisions from the Ch'ing legal code or paraphrases them, for it emerges that the suppression of heterodox cults was in fact official policy starting with the first Ch'ing emperor and continuing thereafter. Under the heading *Prohibition of the Evil Arts of Religious Masters and Shamans* 禁止師巫邪術,[104] various activities of shamans—such as calling down evil spirits, planchette writing, false proclamations of the advent of Maitreya Buddha, and the like, as well as gathering large numbers of people to burn incense at night—are prohibited on pain of death by the garrote for the leaders and lesser penalties for followers. T'ang Pin, therefore, from one point of view, was merely implementing official policy. But the important thing for us is that he was admired for his determination in so doing—and Wu Li shared in that admiration. Efforts by Ch'en Hu and Lu Shih-i—and T'ang Pin himself, as Gernet has noted—to establish associations (*hui*) and covenants (*yüeh*) represented their own attempts to reverse what they considered to be the moral decay of the times.[105]

The second half of Wu Li's poetic couplet ("absolutely no monk's-robes knock at my gate") is also significant. As Ch'en

Yüan puts it in his comment on this line, "For a long time he had cut off relations with Ch'an friends."[106] And Fang Hao too comments that "Yü-shan, before entering the Church, at times had friendships with noble monks. But as of now, 'absolutely no monk's-robes knock at my gate.'"[107] Of Wu Li's "friendships with noble monks," the most important was with a certain Mo-jung 默容 (d. 1672). The chief document for this relationship, as Ch'en Yüan has shown,[108] is an album of ten leaves painted by Wu for Mo-jung in 1666. In the second of his two colophons to this album, dating from 1675 and recorded in the catalog of the collection of P'ang Yüan-chi 龐元濟—the *Hsü-chai ming-hua lu* 虛齋名畫錄—Wu says, "My Ch'an friend Mo-jung followed me [that is, studied with me] in painting, and also set his mind on the study of poetry."[109] In another colophon to this same album, also dating from 1675,[110] Hsü Chih-chien describes the warmth of the friendship between Wu Li and Mo-jung, revealing that whenever Wu visited the Suchou area, he would stay at Mo-jung's Hsing-fu Temple 興福寺. According to Hsü, Wu continued the friendship with Mo-jung's disciple Sheng-yü 聖予, and Hsü himself participated in this relationship. No mention is made in these colophons of any shared interest in Buddhism itself; the relationship is described as based upon the literati arts of poetry and painting. But we must imagine that Wu and Mo-jung spent time discussing Buddhism at the Hsing-fu Temple. How could they have avoided the subject? Like Yang T'ing-yün (or for that matter Chu Hsi and the Ch'eng brothers) before him, Wu must have been interested in Buddhism. But by the age of fifty-nine, and probably before, he had cut off all relations with Buddhist monks and states this fact in a line of verse parallel to one in which he expresses his pleasure at the "extirpation of error" by T'ang Pin.

That Wu Li did reject Buddhism is fully corroborated by two of his comments quoted in a text known variously as *Wu Yü-shan hsien-sheng k'ou-to* 吳漁山先生口鐸, *Hsü k'ou-to jih-ch'ao* 續口鐸日抄, or *Hsü k'ou-to yüeh-ch'ao* 月.[111] This collection of mostly informal comments by Wu Li on the subject of Catholicism, made during the years 1695–1697, was edited by a certain Chao Lun 趙崙—according to Pfister, Wu's catechist and apparently a painter as well.[112] (Chao records the fact that Wu Li praised his painting of the Virgin Mary.) The model for the collection (and the reason for the word *hsü*, "continued," in some versions of the title) was the *K'ou-to jih-ch'ao* by Giulio Aleni, S.J., recording his conversations with Yeh Hsiang-kao 葉向高 (1562–1627), a supporter of Catholic missionaries who never was actually baptized.[113] Two entries in this gathering of Wu Li's sayings make his postconversion (and possibly earlier) position on Buddhism quite clear:[114]

> The Master [Wu Li] questioned me: "There is a man who says to me, 'I do not believe in Buddha, nor do I believe in the Lord of Heaven.' How would you respond to him?" I was unable to answer. The Master said, "All people must have some final foothold—if it is not Heaven, it will be Hell. There is no intermediary void where you can set your feet. If you don't believe in Buddha, fine. But then how can you not believe in the Lord of Heaven?"

> The Master questioned me: "There is a man who says to you, 'I reverence Buddha, and I also reverence the Lord of Heaven.' How would you respond to him?" I was unable to answer. The Master said, "Of the ten thousand creatures beneath heaven, it is man who is noblest. Man is the one among the ten thousand creatures who possesses discernment [*ling* 靈]. If he does not distinguish false from true, in what way is he man? False and true are mutually incompatible, like water and fire; their characteristics are such that they cannot be established together."

Wu Li here adopts the *yü-lu* 語錄 dialogue format favored by Neo-Confucian teachers since Sung times, which was itself influenced in all likelihood by certain teaching techniques and published dialogues of Ch'an masters. He refutes what might be called agnosticism ("I don't believe in anything")—to which he replies that one must believe in something—and indiscriminate ecumenism ("I believe in everything")—to which he replies that one must distinguish between the false and the true (*hsieh cheng* 邪正). One is reminded of Father Brown's response to the claim, "It's your business to believe things." "'Well, I do believe some things, of course,' conceded Father Brown; 'and therefore, of course, I don't believe other things.'"[115]

In taking a position against Buddhism, Wu Li was aligning himself not only with the Jesuits, but with Confucian thinkers such as Ch'en Hu and Lu Shih-i. Where Wu and Ch'en or Lu would have parted company, of course, would have been in the attitude toward Confucianism itself, or at least certain aspects of it. A full study of this question lies beyond the scope of this book. Except for Gernet, scholars such as Julia Ching, Mungello, and Standaert who are now addressing this matter in detail tend to emphasize the compatibility of Confucianism and Christianity for Chinese converts. Wu Li, on the basis of what little we know about his explicit views on this question, may be said to have upheld the Confucian moral order, while questioning Neo-Confucian ontology or metaphysics as well as the cults of certain deities (or apparent deities) in Confucianism.

To address the latter point first, Chao Lun records Wu Li's opinions of Kuan Yü and the brothers Po I and Shu Ch'i 伯夷, 叔齊, who starved rather than eat the grain of the Chou dynasty.[116] When Chao and a fellow student named Ch'en Liang 陳亮 ask Wu for his assessment of Kuan Yü, Wu answers: "Clearly this man openly sold the legitimacy of the Han dynasty to others. He is not worthy to be considered a 'Sage' [*sheng* 聖]." It will be recalled that T'ang Pin, whose suppression of decadent cults Wu approved of, went on to erect a statue precisely of His Holy Highness Lord Kuan 關聖帝君 as a corrective to the spread of false cults. But Wu, while agreeing with T'ang as to the problem, disagreed as to the solution. He may have been influenced by the use of the word *sheng* to translate "saint" in Christianity—he wrote a series of poems in praise of various saints[117]—or by the use of *sheng* in such phrases as *sheng-mu* 聖母 ("Holy Mother," for the Virgin Mary) or *sheng-hui* 會 ("Holy Church"), both expressions used by Wu himself. He may have experienced genuine doubt as to whether Kuan Yü and other venerated figures from history ought properly to be seen as in any way divine. In the case of Po I and Shu Ch'i, he goes so far as to doubt the very historicity of the main incident in the brothers' lives: "We also asked him what sort of men he thought Po I and Shu Ch'i to have been. The Master said, 'Pure. But one simply does not know whether the incident of their plucking ferns at West Mountain and dying of hunger really happened or not.'"

But Wu Li went beyond questioning claims to sanctity on the part of Confucian culture heroes. He took pains to distinguish Neo-Confucian cosmological concepts from Christian terms or ideas that might be confused with them. Without attempting a complete analysis of this complicated matter, let us concentrate on one particularly cogent example: the eleventh poem in the theologically important series of twelve poems entitled "Singing of the Source and Course of Holy Church" (*sung sheng-hui yüan-liu* 誦聖會源流).[118] In partially tentative translation, the poem reads as follows:

> "The Supreme Ultimate contains three"—
>      muddled words indeed!
> In fact, they start with primal energy
>      to speak of original chaos.
> From books of the past, we learned of old
>      of sincerity, wisdom, and goodness;[119]
> the mysterious meaning now we understand
>      of Father, Son, and Holy Spirit.
> The Persons distinct: close at hand, consider
>      the flame within the mirror;
> the Essence is whole: far off, please note
>      the wheel that graces the sky.
> The Holy Name has been revealed
>      His authority conferred;
> throughout the world in this human realm,
>      the sound of the teaching supreme!

Wu Li's immediate concern here appears to be to distinguish the Christian doctrine of the Trinity from confusion with an apparently similar concept in Confucian thought. His first line quotes—with some rearrangement to suit the exigencies of the seven-character meter—a passage in the *Monograph on Pitchpipes and Calendrical Affairs* (*Lü li chih* 律歷志) in the *Han shu* 漢書: "The primal energy of the Supreme Ultimate contains three as one" (*T'ai-chi yüan-ch'i han san wei i* 太極元氣函三為一).[120] The Wei-dynasty annotator Meng K'ang 孟康 explains how one evolves to become three. He further associates "one" with the so-called Yellow Bell—the "fundamental pitch," as Kenneth DeWoskin terms it,[121] from which the others are generated. In describing the *Han shu* formulation as "muddled," Wu Li in his poem intends to distinguish the Christian idea (or rather, revelation) of God as three distinct persons sharing one essence from the idea of a primal unity self-evolving into the multiplicity of the variegated universe. One might go so far as to recognize in this poem an implied rejection of the self-generational model of creation as opposed to the Christian (and Jewish and Islamic) model of creation by a creator. The idea that the universe simply evolved (sometimes with the implication of cyclical repetition) out of a primal unity is of course shared by many archaic systems of thought, as Mircea Eliade has shown, and can even be seen as undergoing a revival in our own time in the formulations of certain cosmologists. In China, the most fully developed version of the model would have been the *T'ai-chi t'u-shuo* 太極圖說 of Chou Tun-i 周敦頤 (1017–1073).[122] But when, in the words of Thomas Molnar, "to the Epicurean theory of all-is-matter, Christian thinkers opposed an extracosmic God, creator of a soul, who did not permeate the universe,"[123] thoughtful men found themselves confronted with two irreconcilable accounts of Creation, between which a choice needed to be made. Wu Li's poem rejects the One becoming the Many, and asserts in its place the revelation of the triune God.

Of course, one might simply say that Wu Li was a Christian when he wrote this poem and when he made the statements in the collection of his religious pronouncements, so of course he put forth Christian doctrine! But the reverse is possible as well (and in my view much more likely): Wu Li, dissatisfied with traditional explanations, found Christian explanations convincing and therefore embraced Christianity in the first place.

Wu Li would presumably have been introduced to Christianity both by Chinese converts and by the Jesuits he himself met, primarily François de Rougemont (1624–1676) and Philippe Couplet (1623–1693), the latter of whom was to invite Wu to accompany him to Rome in 1680 (although Wu would travel only as far as Macao). Lin Xiaoping, drawing on Ch'en Yüan, has convincingly demonstrated that the "Mr. Lu 魯 from the far West" in whose company Wu visited a friend in 1676 according to the inscription on a Shanghai Museum hanging scroll, "Lake in Spring,"[124] was in fact Rougemont. As Lin points out, Ch'en Hu died in 1675, and one might add that Mo-jung had passed away in 1672. The deaths of two men who must have represented Confucianism and Buddhism for him may have rendered Wu more vulnerable to a third influence; or his intellectual and spiritual development at this point may have been such that he was open to such influence. Rougemont in any case was successful in earning the respect of scholar-officials in his day, just as Ricci had been in his. One of the leading poets of the *tz'u* revival, Ch'en Wei-sung 陳維崧 (1625–1682), dedicated one of his ninety-six poems to the tune *The Whole River Is Red* (*man chiang hung* 滿江紅) to Rougemont, as Ch'en Yüan and Lin Xiaoping have both noted:[125]

> To the Foreigner Master Lu from the Far West,
> Again Using the Previous Rhyme Words
> Bizarre! Amazing!
> Oh my, how very fantastic and incredible!
> The places you've passed through:
> noxious vapors of Siam,
> thick fogs of Holland!
> Crane-language: do we know for certain
>     what era it is from?
> Unicorn classics: we do not discern
>     what man wrote them down.
> You rode crashing waves 90,000 *li* to come,
> sea turtles your companions.
> Ocean beyond oceans—
> light like lacquer!
> Country beyond countries—
> sky with no sun.
> They speak of dwarf-lands and giants:
> The soul shakes, limbs tremble!
> Good at chess—accustomed to raking in
>     the venerable immortal's oranges;

skilled at medicine—you laugh
  at the herbs of Shen Nung.
And then you chant through a book of spells on people:
  we're startled by your strange arts.

Ch'en Wei-sung seems almost to have regarded Rougemont as a kind of educated freak, a fascinating but ultimately alien exhibit at a sideshow. Wu Li was impressed by much more than Rougemont's medical or chess-playing skills, and realized that his liturgical texts were more than "spells." The "wise man from the West," to borrow Vincent Cronin's phrase for Ricci,[126] came bearing answers to the very questions that were being debated in the circles where Wu Li was accustomed to move. The one dilemma we cannot solve is why one Confucian literatus—Wu Li—responded to the deeper message carried by Rougemont and his colleagues, while another—Ch'en Wei-sung—was merely intrigued and amused. The answer to that question lies secreted, as implied by Willard Peterson, in precisely those depths of the soul not accessible to scholarship.

# 3

# Wu Li's Christian Poetry

Influenced by the Sung-poetry revival of the early Ch'ing and by Wang Shih-chen's "metaphysical" school of poetry—and, as well, a committed convert to Catholicism who understood clearly the distinctions between Christian doctrine and Confucian, Taoist, or Buddhist doctrine—Wu Li was prepared to undertake his bold attempt to create something totally new in Chinese literature: a Chinese Christian poetry. That Wu Li did so with full consciousness of what he was doing is suggested by a brief but significant remark he made to Chao Lun: "Writing poems of the Heavenly Learning [*t'ien-hsüeh shih* 天學詩] is the most difficult thing. It cannot be compared to the writing of other poetry."[127] Heavenly Learning, as many scholars have pointed out, sometimes was used as a general term for the teachings of the Jesuits, including their scientific teachings as well as Catholicism.[128] But there can be no question that Wu Li here is referring specifically to Catholicism. Earlier in this entry, Chao Lun records Wu Li's praise for Chao's own poetry: "I have just read your poems; they are extremely fine." To this, Chao replies with a promise to have them printed next year and presented to Wu Li, if Wu would first correct them. But Wu says they have no flaws, and presents Chao with a rosary and a cross. Chao's poems may well have been religious in nature, and thus may have stimulated Wu's remark; perhaps Wu's experiment in writing the new poetry was shared with his disciples. But after making the remark, "he then took out his poems 'Eastern Tower' and 'Inscribed on the Feng-ah Mountain Residence [and Presented to Hou Ta-nien]' as well as the poems presented to him by various famous men and gave them to me to read. After chanting them for a long time, I withdrew." The two poems mentioned by Chao are neither of them Christian in nature;[129] still less, of course, would have been the poems presented to Wu Li by Wang Shih-chen and colleagues. Apparently Wu still took pride in his conventional poetry and was not prepared for whatever reason to follow his remark as might be expected by showing Chao examples of his own Christian poetry. Was Wu dissatisfied with his efforts in this new area and therefore not yet ready to show his experimental works even to his catechist?

Wu Li's poetry can be divided into four broad groupings:

1. Wu Li's "conventional" poems—that is, *shih* poems virtually indistinguishable from similar poems by his contemporaries or for that matter from countless traditional Chinese poems on standard themes. Such poems constitute the bulk of MCSC, and Wu probably continued to write poems of this type in his later years as well.

2. What might be considered a transitional group of thirty quatrains in seven-character meter on life in Macao. These poems do touch on Christian themes, mostly in the context of a broad portrait of the customs and festivals of the Portuguese community. The first two leaves of Wu Li's holograph album of these poems are reproduced here as Plate 4.

3. *Shih* poems fully devoted to Christian themes. These poems—about eighty of them—are found immediately after the Macao poems in the *San-pa chi* 三巴集 (the title is a partial transliteration of São Paulo or St. Paul, the name of the Jesuit church in Macao where Wu Li studied), in the edition of the MCC, chap. 3; in other editions, *San-pa chi* is limited to the Macao poems, the Christian poems having been excised by certain editors, presumably because of their hostility to Christianity. Some poems of this type are also found in the *San-yü chi*, interspersed with "conventional" poems.[130]

4. A book of *ch'ü* poems entitled "Compendium of Orthodox Sounds of Heavenly Music" (*T'ien yüeh cheng yin p'u* 天樂正音譜), listed by Pfister (apparently erroneously) as forming part of MCC,[131] but actually a manuscript recovered by Fang Hao in 1946 from the Zikawei library and printed by him with the help of *ch'ü* scholars Lu

Ch'ien 盧前 and Cheng Ch'ien 鄭騫 in 1950, and then again with more extensive notes in 1968.[132] These poems—some describing the Mass, some in praise of the Virgin Mary, others recounting or even dramatizing moments in the Old Testament, and some purely theological—represent the culmination of Wu Li's experiment in creating a Chinese Christian poetry. They may have been difficult to write; they are certainly difficult to understand, and the discussion of them here must be tentative and preliminary.

Wu Li's poems of the first type, conventional poems in a vaguely Sung manner including many *t'i-hua shih* 題畫詩 ("poems-inscribed-on-paintings"),[133] are not without value; one can in fact derive much enjoyment from them. But if Wu Li had written only these poems, he would not have merited special study as a poet, let alone a place in the history of Chinese literature. It is therefore the poems of the next three types that are discussed here.

When another poet, Gerard Manley Hopkins, became a Jesuit, he struggled with the conflict between the desire to write poetry and the strict Jesuit regimen, which may include actual strictures on writing which is not purely devotional in nature, as it did for periods of time in Hopkins's case. It is unclear whether Wu Li himself was ever formally placed under orders to avoid poetry or painting, but in one of the thirty quatrains on life in Macao (poem 28), he certainly reveals an inner conflict. This poem bears a prose note by Wu which proudly states, "I have received firm permission to study the Way":

As one grows old, who can bring back
    the time when he was young?
I work so hard, day after day,
    but fear I'm much too slow.
I think of my old practice,
    wish to burn up my inkstone
and then stop smearing crow-marks
    and give up poetry.[134]

But Wu Li did not give up poetry. His Macao sequence, *Ao-chung tsa-yung* 嶴中雜詠, consisting of thirty quatrains with seven

characters per line, may well be the first poems in Chinese literature to describe Western customs in some detail on the basis of
direct observation. The book bears two prefaces,[135] the first by
Sung Shih-ying 宋實穎 (1621–1705). Sung praises Wu for his poetry, painting, and calligraphy (in that order) and then inexplic-
ably claims that "recently he has further devoted his mind to the
School of the Mind [*hsin-hsüeh* 心學]." Possibly Sung intended this
term to stand for Catholicism, rather than for the Wang Yang-
ming 王陽明 (1472–1529) branch of Neo-Confucianism against
which Wu's teacher Ch'en Hu was in revolt.

More significant is the second of the two prefaces, that by the
poet, dramatist, and scholar Yu T'ung.[136] Although brief, this text
is important and worth translating in full:

> When I was in the Bureau of History compiling the *Account
> of Foreign Countries* [*wai-kuo chuan* 外國傳],[137] I perceived
> that the foreign countries' customs are bizarre and strange,
> and in my mind I greatly marveled at this. I therefore
> wrote one hundred "Bamboo Branch Songs" to record some-
> thing of them.[138] In the present case, the Ao-shan [Macao]
> of which Master Wu Yü-shan sings is no further away than
> the Hundredfold Yüeh 粵 region [Kuangchou province],
> and yet it is a center for foreign tribute-marketing, so that
> what one's ears and eyes encounter there is frequently dif-
> ferent from ordinary experience. Should Tzu-yün return to
> life, he would certainly "prepare writing silk" and go to record
> the language there.[139] But I regret that I have not gotten to
> prepare this material [that is, to go to Macao]. Master Wu
> is elegantly skillful at poetry and excellent at calligraphy
> and painting. Recently he has returned from beyond the
> sea, and his words in these poems are crisp and clear, with
> the zest of one who has ridden the wind. I marvel at this
> especially, and I too wish to "cling to the sleeve" of the
> "magician."

Ch'en Yüan dates this preface to 1690,[140] by which time Wu
would have returned from Macao. It is unclear whether Yu T'ung
actually believed that Wu Li had gone as far as Rome with Couplet and then returned, or saw Macao, even though close by in
terms of actual geography, as a virtual foreign land, "beyond the

sea" figuratively if not literally. In either case, there is no mistaking his envy at Wu's achievement of describing foreign customs in poetry on the basis of eyewitness observation, as opposed to the descriptions of French or Dutch customs in his own "Bamboo Branch Songs on Foreign Countries,"[141] which were based merely on accounts in books. Yu ends with a telling allusion to the passage in *Lieh Tzu* describing the dream journey to heaven of King Mu (in Graham's rendition): "In the time of King Mu of Chou, there came from a country in the far West a *magician*. . . . He invited the King to come with him on an excursion. He soared upwards, with King Mu *clinging to his sleeve*."[142] It is unlikely to be a coincidence that, as we have seen, Ch'en Hu's disciple Ch'ü Yu-chung (in his poem "Music of Harmonious Heaven"), Wu Li himself (in the fifth poem from his series "Moved to Sing of the Truth of Holy Church"), and now Yu T'ung all allude to this same episode in *Lieh Tzu:* The fact that the "magician" (*hua-jen* 化人) comes from the far West must somehow have seemed to them—at least to Wu Li and Yu T'ung—a prophetic foreshadowing of the arrival of the recent visitors from the far West, visitors with seemingly magical skill at foretelling eclipses and—more important—visitors who, like Lieh Tzu's magician, held out the promise of access to Heaven.

When Couplet invited Wu Li to accompany him to Rome, the invitation would not have seemed as inconceivable as might appear. Couplet had spent a two-year period between 1669 and 1671 in Canton living with or near Cheng Wei-hsin 鄭維信 (1633–1673), also known by his Portuguese baptismal name of Emmanuel de Siqueira.[143] Emmanuel's father, "Antonio de Siqueira," had already converted to Catholicism, and so his son was baptized at birth. As Rouleau has shown, when Fr. Alexandre de Rhodes, "veteran of the Cochin China and Tonkin missions...set sail from Macao for Europe on 20 December 1645," the twelve-year-old Emmanuel de Siqueira was on board. At one point during the journey, to escape capture by Turks who took him for a "disguised Tartar Moslem," de Siqueira was hidden in an Armenian Dominican monastery where he lived for six months, becoming fluent in

Armenian. He arrived in Rome in 1650 and proceeded on a course of Jesuit education at the Collegio Romano which involved rhetoric, logic, natural theology, and metaphysics (1653–1657). From 1657 to 1660 he actually taught the classics in this college as professor of "Grammatica" and "Litterae humaniores." In 1660, he transferred to Bologna and pursued theological studies there, eventually completing them at Coimbra, where he earned cum laude status and was raised to the priesthood, probably in 1664, to become the first Chinese Jesuit priest. He returned to China in 1668—twenty-three years after his departure from Macao—and needed to take a refresher course in Chinese; he had gotten rusty in his native tongue. His activities as a priest were limited to the Kuangtung area, where he would have met Couplet.

De Siqueira's success in adapting to European culture and in pursuing the comprehensive course of Jesuit studies stands in stark contrast to the failure of the far less significant "John Hu" recently featured in a book by Jonathan Spence.[144] Indeed, it must have inspired Couplet to attempt the sponsorship of a second Chinese Jesuit: Wu Li seemed suitable for the role. But when Couplet embarked from Macao on December 4 or 5, 1681, Wu Li remained in Macao and, entering the Society of Jesus, pursued his studies there, culminating in ordination as a priest, together with two other Chinese Jesuits, at the hand of the Chinese Dominican bishop (the first Chinese bishop, in fact), Lo Wen-tsao 羅文藻 (Gregory Lopez; d. 1691), on August 1, 1688.

In the first of the thirty Macao poems, Wu Li triumphantly proclaims his reason for coming to the "City of the Holy Name of God of Macao in China," which had been visited by Portuguese ships as early as 1517, and since the mid-sixteenth century had functioned as a sort of quasi-official trading post for the Portuguese, achieving "city" status around 1585 and continuing thereafter as a community of Portuguese and Chinese residents, some at least of the latter Christian converts:

> At the pass, Kuang-tung ends,
>     then down to level sand;
> mountain formations at Hao-ching
>     can be compared to flowers.

Residents! Don't be alarmed!
I'm not here by mistake.
From afar I've come to study the Way
at São Paulo Church!

Wu Li adds a prose note: "The mountain colors are purplish-black, their forms comparable to flower buds. São Paulo is the name of the church of the Society of Jesus." The first couplet of this quatrain (as well as the first part of the note) reveals the influence of the Sung-poetry movement: the careful attention to the actual lay of the land—in a word, the realism. Wu's poetry teacher, Ch'ien Ch'ien-i, concerned that travel writing, whether prose or poetry, should be based on actual experience of a place, attempted in his poems on the Yellow Mountains, for example, to convey such experience and "sense of place."[145] This concept in turn was consistent with calls by late-Ming Kung-an writers for a poetry reflecting the characteristics of real places, as Tu Fu's Szechwan poetry captured the special feel of the Szechwan landscape.

The residents Wu Li strives to reassure (in the third line of this poem) consisted—at least in 1635 when Antonio Bocarro, Chronicler-in-Chief of the State of India, wrote his detailed account of Macao (without actually having visited there)—of some 850 Portuguese families with "on the average about six slaves capable of bearing arms, amongst whom the majority and the best are negroes and such like," as well as a like number of "native families, including Chinese Christians . . . who form the majority [of the non-Portuguese residents] and other nations, all Christians."[146] (Bocarro may have been mistaken in declaring that all the Chinese in Macao were Christians.)

Wu Li, like Bocarro, noted the presence in Macao both of black slaves and of non-Han Chinese such as the Tanka boat people, and in the third poem of his sequence he combines references to these two groups:

Yellow sand, whitewashed houses: here the black men live;
willows at the gates like sedge, still not sparse in autumn.

Midnight's when the Tanka come and make their harbor here;
fasting kitchens for noonday meals have plenty of fresh fish.

[Poet's note:] The blacks by custom admire a deep black color as beautiful; a pale black they consider ugly. There are two varieties of fish: shad
and *liu* fish. They are fried in Western olive oil, and then eaten for the
forty-day lenten fast.

Again, the attempt to describe the actual Macao scene is evident
in the first two lines; Wu Li has also observed that the blacks had
separate living quarters. The second half of the poem unfolds a
scene of Tanka boat people bringing in fish to supply the needs of
fasting Christians. In his tightly packed note at the end, Wu plays
amateur anthropologist in his claim that the blacks prefer a darker
shade of skin color; identifies two types of fish; and calls attention
to a Mediterranean culinary tradition: the frying of fish in olive oil.
Finally, he refers to the important Christian practice of the lenten
fast forty days prior to Holy Week leading to Easter. One senses a
man nearly overwhelmed with fascinating new experiences and
eager to capture them in poetry. Nothing could be more different
from the usual view of later Chinese poetry as moribund repeti-
tions of old formulas.

The religious practices of the Portuguese and other Christians at
Macao were, of course, of particular interest to Wu Li, and his
fourth poem provides the first detailed, firsthand account in
Chinese literature (perhaps the only such account) of a Christian
procession of the sort that continues to play a central role in the
religious life of Mediterranean countries:

Holding candles, burning high,
    they welcome the great saint;
banners, pennants flap in wind,
    cannon roar like thunder.
On all sides streets are spread with grass,
    green like tapestry:
pedestrians are not allowed to trample it to dust.

[Poet's note:] When St. Francis Xavier [1506–1552] emerges in procession, the streets are covered with flowers and grass to show reverence. The
streets are called "Awe of Majesty, Love of Virtue."

Every detail in this poem is, of course, new; Wu Li could not draw upon centuries of crystallized conventional phrases as he could in the case of his preconversion poems about visits to Buddhist temples, farewells to friends departing on official duties, or paintings of fishermen. Writing at a time when Chinese poetry is often thought to have declined in originality, Wu is compelled to create fresh diction in order "to depict a scene that is difficult to describe in such a way that it seems to be right before the eyes of the reader." There simply was no precedent for "cannon roar like thunder," or "candles" to "welcome the great saint." Although technically on Chinese soil, Wu Li here established himself as the first Chinese poet to describe accurately Western customs as an eyewitness; Yu T'ung's envy, expressed in his preface, is understandable.

The twenty-seventh poem of the series describes another important Christian custom, the construction of elaborate crèches at Christmas. The Portuguese-style "winter mountains" (as Wu Li calls them) built in Macao seem to have been particularly elaborate and were apparently the focus of festive celebrations with music and dance:

A thousand lanterns glitter from a cliff of tiny trees:
brocades forming cloudy peaks, candles forming flowers.
They decorate these winter mountains and all come to enjoy:
black men's dancing feet keep time to the guitar!

[Poet's note:] The winter mountains are made of wood formed into the underlying rock, brocaded cloth as mountain peaks, dyed candles of red and blue as flowers and trees. In form it is like a tortoise mountain. When the blacks sing, they move their feet in a dance which keeps time with the sounds of the guitar. This all takes place around the time of Jesus's birth.

In his lengthy note to this poem, Wu Li describes in detail the construction of the "winter mountains" and compares them to Chinese "tortoise mountains"—constructions for the display of lanterns at the Lantern Festival and on other occasions.

Wu Li did not limit himself to the role of observer in Macao. He interacted with Portuguese residents and in certain of the Macao poems describes his impressions of their behavior. The ninth poem, for example, opens with a typical couplet of landscape description but goes on to conjure up a vignette of Wu drinking wine and discussing with Portuguese acquaintances the differing customs of their two countries. He was particularly impressed, it seems, by the Western custom of removing the hat as a sign of greeting:

> The palm trees here provide thick shade,
>     the place is never cold;
> the birds sing when the springtime comes,
>     the wineshops fill with cheer.
> All visitors drink wine and talk
>     of things in native lands;
> the etiquette is much the same,
>     except—they doff their hats!

[Poet's note:] Those who wear their hair in a hanging bun with gold threads favor a hat of black flannel wool; this hat is shaped like a bamboo *li*-hat. When they meet someone they doff it as a greeting.

Wu's efforts at communication with the Portuguese continued late at night and involved recourse to writing when Wu's command of Portuguese (or Latin), or his companion's command of Chinese, proved inadequate; but then the writing too would be difficult, as Wu good-heartedly complains in the twenty-sixth poem of the sequence:

> In lamplight, our native tongues, one West and one East:
> when we don't understand, we can still use the brush
>     and thus converse.
> I write my fly-head words and you, your words
>     like legs of flies;
> read horizontally or vertically, so hard to penetrate!

[Poet's note:] The Western characters are like fly-legs; they are written horizontally. In reading them out loud, a sharp, high pitch is considered best.

Wu Li was clearly entranced by the new world to which he had gained access in Macao. But he still thought of Couplet, en route to Rome across the sea. Did he yearn to follow him some day?

### 10

> Windswept ship, dashing quickly,
>     day and night with dizzy speed:
> who could lie secure in it, dreaming of his homeland?

The itinerary lies ahead—passage to the distant West!
Today they must have gone beyond the Crimson Path.

[Poet's note:] In reckoning Master Couplet's itinerary, I would estimate
that he must have crossed the Crimson Path [Equator].

Wu Li's pioneering poetic sequence on Macao apparent'y inspired Ch'ü Ta-chün—the poet and scholar who had converted to
Buddhism and then back again to Confucianism—to write a much
shorter sequence of his own entitled *Ao-men* 澳門 and consisting of
seven poems.[147] Judging from their position in his collected works,
they must date from 1689 or early 1690. The five-character
regulated-verse poems like Wu's are filled with details of Macao
life—the ships, the "red-haired" foreigners, the roses held by the
"barbarian" women, the cannon, the telescope—but Ch'ü is at
least as suspicious of the foreign presence as he is intrigued by it.
Several references are made to the problem posed for the Chinese
authorities by the presence on their borders of this enclave of
potential troublemakers: "Foreign countries here frequently pick
fights; / the Westerners for a long time have hidden troops in
ambush. / Our soldiers grieve that barbarian weapons are so
cleverly made." "One day, barbarian merchants occupied this
place; / for a thousand years since, Han generals have been kept
busy." Ch'ü seems to have had only the vaguest idea of the religion of Macao. In an essay which he also wrote about the place,
he relates:

> One of their temples [*szu* 寺] is called San-pa. It is over one
> hundred feet tall, like a stone tower, and is very lavishly
> carved. They worship Jesus as the Lord of Heaven and this is
> where he resides. A monk [*seng* 僧] known as the King of
> the Law [*fa-wang* 法王] is in charge of their sect. Any for-
> eigner who has committed a sin comes to the temple. If the
> King of the Law does not permit him to repent, he is im-
> mediately punished by execution. But if he is permitted to re-
> pent, he himself cuts his body with iron hooks until his blood
> flows everywhere. Thus he believes he may escape the calam-
> ity of Hell. Men and women day and night repair to the tem-
> ple to worship, and to listen to discourses of the monks.[148]

Ch'ü goes on to describe the organ, praising its music, as well as other treasures of Western science such as a telescope, a microscope, and a "glass thousand-man mirror," a "many-treasured mirror" which transforms the image of a single man into hundreds of men. Like Wu Li, he notes the custom of doffing the hat. On the whole, Ch'ü's attitude is the familiar one of fascination with Western science mingled with skepticism about the religion—depicted here almost as if it were one of the lewd cults suppressed by T'ang Pin—and suspiciousness of Western intentions. By comparison, Wu Li's poems are astonishingly empathetic and free of xenophobia.

The Macao poems, as extraordinary as they are, limit their references to Catholicism to what might anachronistically be termed the anthropological perspective; the processions, crèches, church bells, and other phenomena mentioned in the poems could be seen simply as threads in the broader cultural tapestry. The only poem in the sequence which might conceivably be interpreted as making a theological point would be the thirteenth:

> Where trees encircle the Three Mountains
>     herbs grow fragrantly;
> how could they lead to the confounding
>     of several sovereign lords?
> Left behind by the Ch'in gatherers
>     still they flourish, green:
> the herbs themselves achieved Long Life,
>     the men are long since gone!
>
> [Poet's note:] Three Mountains is traditionally said to be the spot where herbs were plucked in the Ch'in and Han periods.

This dig at the type of Taoism that involved the search for immortality through concoctions of herbs, alchemical procedures, and the like would have earned the sympathy of Yüan Yu-pai, the classmate of Lu Shih-i who rejected *hsien* 仙 Taoism for Buddhism, but this poem too forms part of a venerable tradition of poems casting doubt on the use of herbs in the search for longevity, going back at least as far as certain poems by T'ao Ch'ien (the poet from whom Ch'en Yü-chi claimed Wu Li's poetry derived) and reaching its fullest development in the New Yüeh-fu poems of Po

Chü-i, one of which—"The Ocean is Wide" (*Hai man-man* 海漫漫)—deals with this theme.

Wu Li's truly theological poems in the *shih* form, the next major group to be considered, themselves may be aligned along a spectrum from poems in which the religious theme is introduced quite subtly to those which are thoroughly Catholic from the first word. As an example of a poem in which the Christian theme is only introduced toward the end, let us consider the "Song of the Fisherman" (*Yü-fu yin* 漁父吟) from the *San-yü chi*.[149] This poem may be seen as a brilliant variation on the age-old fisherman theme in Chinese poetry and painting, a theme, moreover, of which Wu himself was a master. Before turning to the "Song," it might be useful to read two conventional fisherman poems by Wu, both of them inscribed on paintings of his. The first is the twenty-first *t'i-hua shih* in the series of forty which ends the MCSC:

> Moistening the green, misty clouds
> fly above, below:
> these wooded mountains look just like
> a painting by Mi Yu-jen.
> Astonishing! Splashed ink creates
> a storm of wind and rain;
> wildly it buffets the fishing boat,
> at evening not yet home.[150]

The conceit that this painted scene is an actual place in nature which reminds the viewer of a painting (by Mi Yu-jen 米友仁 [1072–1151], famous together with his father Mi Fu 米芾 [1052–1107] for the use of moist black "dots" to evoke scenes of mist and rain), however charming, is in fact thoroughly conventional in *t'i-hua shih*, as is the understated presence of the fishing boat, introduced only in the last line and with no reference to the fisherman himself at all. By contrast, although still well within the realm of convention, we may consider another seven-character quatrain inscribed on a hanging scroll of 1675 by Wu Li in ink and colors on paper once in the collection of the great Japanese painter Tomioka Tessai 富岡鐵齋 (1836–1924),[151] a quatrain apparently uncollected in any of Wu Li's printed writings. Although the words "fisher-man" or "fishing" do not occur in the poem, the context of both the poem and the painted scene indicate that we are in the realm of the fisherman theme:

> My hermit's life, entirely passed within a single boat!
> I ask the world for nothing, I only love pure calm.
> I cast far off through rivers and lakes
>     so I can read in peace,
> yet ears and eyes still feel hemmed in
>     by all these verdant mountains.

This again is the classic theme of the hermit-fisherman (a lite-ratus in this case who wants to "read in peace"), pictured sitting in his moored boat at the bottom of the painting, in search of "pure calm"; given such a conventional theme, however, Wu Li rings a subtle variation. This fisherman's desire for tranquility is so strong that he feels hemmed in even by the green mountains and hopes to find a spot still more quiet than the already idyllic landscape he inhabits in this painting.

But the variation of the fisherman theme in Wu Li's "Song of the Fisherman" is radical:

> From patching rips in tattered nets
>     his eyes have gotten blurred;
> he scours the river, does not disdain
>     the tiniest fish and shrimp.
> Selecting the freshest, he has supplied
>     the feasts of sovereigns;
> all four limbs exhausted now,
>     dare he refuse the work?
> Spreading nets he gets confused
>     by water just like sky;
> song lingering, still drunk, approaches
>     dragons as they sleep.
> Now hair and whiskers are all white,
>     his face has aged with time;
> he's startled by the wind and waves
>     and fears an early autumn.

Some friends of his have changed their jobs:
   they now are fishers of men;
he hears, compared to fishing fish,
   this task is tougher still.
Of late he finds the Heavenly Learning
   has come into the city:
to customers now happily add families that fast.

The first eight lines of this twelve-line poem could be a version of the traditional theme, although the emphasis on the fisherman's exhaustion and the hardship of his labors would be unusual; indeed, in fisherman poems in general a literatus-recluse is more often intended than a professional fisherman. But, like Simon Peter and Andrew, this man is a real fisherman. And, also like them, friends of his at least (if not himself) have changed their profession—and have become "fishers of men" (Matthew 4:19). They have "left their nets" (Matthew 4:20) to follow Jesus. "James the son of Zebedee and John his brother, in a ship with Zebedee their father, mending their nets" (Matthew 4:21) were also called; Wu's fisherman at the beginning of the poem is "patching rips in tattered nets." "All four limbs exhausted now," will he too change profession? For now, he is content to discover that the Heavenly Learning has brought him new business—customers that eat fish during periods of fasting.

The contrast between Wu Li's two types of fisherman is crucial. One seeks "rest in Nature"; the other may soon find rest in the "God of Nature," to use the expressions of a poet who died one year after Wu Li was born, George Herbert (1593–1633). In "The Pulley,"[152] Herbert clarifies the distinction, which is of key importance for a Christian like Herbert or Wu Li. "When God at first made men," he held "rest" in reserve:

   For if I should (said he)
Bestow this jewel also on my creature,
He would adore my gifts instead of me,
And rest in Nature, not the God of Nature:
   So both should losers be.

   Yet let him keep the rest,
But keep them with repining restlessness:

> Let him be rich and weary, that at least,
> If goodness lead him not, yet weariness
>         May toss him to my breast.

The fisherman of the poem on the painting from the Tessai collection seeks "pure calm," yet still feels "hemmed in" by the green mountains and so must continue to "cast far off," again reminiscent of Herbert in "The Collar,"[153] where he cries, ". . . No more. / I will abroad. / What? Shall I ever sigh and pine? / My lines and life are free; free as the rode, / Loose as the wind, as large as store," but finds only agitation, until "Me thoughts I heard one calling, *Child:* / And I replied, *My Lord.*" In one of the great modern accounts of a conversion experience, C. S. Lewis's *Surprised by Joy,* Lewis begins one of his chapters—"I Broaden My Mind"— with the opening lines of "The Collar."[154] Wu Li's fisherman too hovers on the brink of realization that ultimately rest is not to be found in Nature; this realization radically separates Wu from mainstream Chinese culture or indeed from any culture that seeks final repose in the creation as opposed to the Creator. The "Song of the Fisherman" fulfills the insight; it is one of Wu's most successful poems, a triumphant bridge between two different uses of a single image, with profound theological implications.

In other poems, Wu describes aspects of his own life as priest, busy with the task of administering sacraments such as baptism. "Sent to Kuo" is a poem of congratulation to a man who has recently received this sacrament (whether at Wu Li's own hand or someone else's is not clear):

> The gate of eternal blessings
>         this day has opened for you;
> the light of grace and felicitation
>         have come to you from Heaven.
> Extirpated are your former taints,
>         repulsed the Devil's troops;
> now you will enjoy the real bread,
>         formed in the Holy Womb.
> How dignified! Your name has entered
>         the register of the righteous.

How glorious! Your heart
    becomes an altar for the Lord.

I know you will prove worthy
    to console the people's yearning;

the great hall now is in need of pillars
    raised on rock.[155]

As Li Ti indicates in a brief note, "We do not know Kuo's personal name, nor do we know where he came from. At the time, he had received baptism and taken the Holy Bread [the Eucharist]. The Master [Wu Li] wrote this poem to congratulate him." Kuo was presumably one of the common people who formed the bulk of converts; even so, Wu seems to urge him in the last two lines of this eight-line regulated verse to become a priest himself. Wu skillfully manipulates the new terminology to achieve the parallelism called for in regulated verse: "Devil's troops" is paralleled by "Holy Womb." The sacrament of baptism, of course, includes formulas for the renunciation of the Devil; the idea that the "real bread" was formed in the Virgin's womb is also theologically sound; the body of Christ took shape in her womb, and the real bread is in fact his body. The idea that the sacrament has opened the "gate" to Heaven is consistent with Wu's interest in imagery of Heaven and access to Heaven, as we shall see.

Wu Li's most ambitious *shih* poems on theological themes are those arranged in two sequences of nine and twelve poems respectively: "Moved to Sing of the Truth of Holy Church" and "Singing of the Source and Course of Holy Church."[156] The second of these sequences especially is one of Wu Li's highest poetic achievements, and perhaps the most successful attempt in his *oeuvre* to create a Chinese Christian poetry. The poems are eight-line regulated verse, seven characters per line, combining ecstatic descriptions of a paradisiacal Heaven (sometimes almost Islamic in their voluptuousness) with references to the Creation, the Incarnation, the Crucifixion, and trinitarian theology. The eleventh poem, which contrasts the Neo-Confucian (and Taoist) idea of the One evolving into the Many with the revelation of the Christian Trinity, has already been analyzed. Like "Sent to Kuo," certain of the remaining poems are at the far end of the spectrum from "Song of the

Fisherman" in that their religious or theological character is immediately evident from the first line.

The first poem in the series reads as follows:

> Within the twelvefold walled enclosure,
>     at the highest spot
> is the palace of the Lord
>     with springs and autumns of its own.
> The misty fragrance is breath of flowers
>     where roses bloom;
> the glittering brilliance is glow of pearls
>     where gemmed crowns reverently bow.
> There in Heaven should we seek
>     true blessings and true joy;
> in the human realm we must cut off
>     false strivings and false plans.
> Look there where girls, so many of them,
>     their hair in tufts,
> day after day follow behind
>     the Holy Mother in their play.

This is one of several poems in these two sequences in which Wu Li tries to evoke the atmosphere of Heaven. He combines traditional Chinese expressions from the classics—which after all contain many descriptions of heavenly palaces or paradises on the moon, in the sky, or hidden away somewhere in the mountains or in caves—with new expressions created either by himself or by Jesuit translators. One of these in the present poem appears to be *chu-kung* 主宮, "the palace of the Lord," in the second line. The second couplet conjures up a sensuous Heaven closer to the paradise of Islam than to ordinary Christian imagery, although the "glittering brilliance" of "gemmed crowns reverently bowing," and indeed the whole setting with the gates of the heavenly palace, is vaguely reminiscent of Revelation 4–5 ("Behold, a door was opened in heaven," and so forth), a section of the Bible also echoed in other poems in both sequences. The presence of the Virgin in paradise, surrounded by young girls, is consistent with depictions in Christian art. For example, the visionary Cretan icon painter, Georgios Klontzas (ca. 1540–1608), in his magnificent Last Judgment triptych,[157] shows the Virgin (together with Abraham) in paradise surrounded by children and angelic musicians; below, the blessed are welcomed into paradise—depicted here with theological justification as the Garden of Eden now redeemed—by Christ as Priest, serving them the Eucharist. (Klontzas's work was famous in Western Europe, and he accepted commissions from Catholic patrons.)

2

Before the firmament was ever formed,
    or any foundation laid,
high there hovered the Judge of the World,
    prepared for the last days!
This single Man from His five wounds
    poured every drop of blood;
a myriad nations gave their hearts
    to the wonder of the Cross!
The heavenly gates now have a ladder
    leading to their peace:
demonic spirits lack any art
    to insinuate deception.
Take up the burden, joyfully
    fall in behind Jesus,
look up with reverence towards the top of that mountain,
    follow His every step.

Jacques Gernet, in his influential book *China and the Christian Impact—a Conflict of Cultures*, writes: "It is . . . worth noting that the seventeenth-century Chinese Christians never make any allusion to Jesus in their writings, limiting themselves to paying homage to the Sovereign on High, or *shangdi*."[158] This, he claims, is because they did not know of "an opposition between a transcendent eternity and a worldly transitoriness, between the two of which, precisely, [the Incarnation] operates as a mediator." But in the first poem of this series, seventeenth-century Chinese Christian Wu Li devotes his third couplet precisely to a contrastive parallel between "Heaven"—where "true joy" is to be sought—and the "human realm" characterized by "false strivings." And in the present poem, he not only speaks of Christ but specifically refers to "His five wounds" and the blood that flowed from them on the Cross. Such imagery had never appeared in Chinese poetry before. One is reminded of medieval meditations on the blood and wounds of Christ. The actual name of Jesus appears in the penultimate line.

Did Wu Li know of the Incarnation as a "mediator" between the transcendent and earthly realms? Line 5 of the present poem proves that he did: "The heavenly gates now have a ladder leading to their peace" (*ch'ang-ho yu t'i t'ung tan-tang* 閶闔有梯通淡蕩). The term *ch'ang-ho* for "heavenly gates" originally occurred in the *Li sao* 離騷 (lines 207–208): *"wu ling ti-hun k'ai kuan hsi / i ch'ang-ho erh wang yü"* 吾令帝閽開關兮倚閶闔而望予.[159] This Hawkes translates: "I asked Heaven's porter to open up for me; / But he leant across Heaven's gate and eyed me churlishly."[160]

The *Ch'u tz'u* 楚辭 anthology also provides the locus classicus for the expression *t'ien-t'i* 天梯, "heavenly ladder" (Wu Li uses the word *t'i* alone), in the poem *Shang shih* 傷時, "Distressed by These Times" (Hawkes) in the *Chiu ssu* 九思 sequence. The lines in question (lines 35–36) read as follows: *"yüan t'ien-t'i hsi pei shang / teng t'ai-i hsi yü t'ai"* 緣天梯兮北上，登太一兮玉臺.[161] Hawkes renders these lines, "Then, ascending heaven's ladder, I mounted the northern sky, / Climbed the jade terrace of the King of Heaven."[162] The use of a ladder to ascend to the sky is appropriate in the shamanistic atmosphere of the *Ch'u tz'u*, and indeed there exist throughout the world "countless examples of shamanic ascent to the sky by means of a ladder,"[163] as Mircea Eliade has demonstrated. But Eliade notes as well that "the mystical ladder is abundantly documented in Christian tradition,"[164] and the locus would, of course, be the vision of Jacob (Genesis 28:12–13):

> And he dreamed, and behold a ladder set up on the earth, and the top of it reached to heaven: and behold the angels of God ascending and descending on it. And, behold, the Lord stood above it. . . .

Early Christian writers were quick to interpret the ladder as a foreshadowing or symbol of the Cross. St. Irenaeus (d. ca. 202),

Bishop of Lyons, sometime late in the second century wrote in his *Proof of the Apostolic Preaching*:

> Jacob also, while journeying into Mesopotamia, sees Him, in a dream, standing at the ladder, that is, the tree [the Cross], set up from earth even to heaven, for by it those who believe in Him mount to heaven, for His passion is our raising on high. And all visions of this kind signify the Son of God.[165]

The fullest development of this imagery is in *The Ladder of Divine Ascent* by St. John Climacus (ca. 579–649),[166] abbot of the monastery of St. Katherine at Mount Sinai. In this work, one of the greatest Christian devotional books ever written, St. John unfolds an elaborate parallel between ascent rung by rung to Heaven and the progressive overcoming of the deadly sins. Enormously influential throughout Christendom, the book was translated from the original Greek into many Eastern languages: Syriac, Arabic, and the Armenian learned by Emmanuel de Siqueira. Latin translations were produced in the eleventh century, and in the thirteenth or early fourteenth by the Franciscan Angelus Clarenus.[167] Icon and wall paintings of the ladder often show it culminating at a pair of gates which swing open to reveal Christ, who leans forward to welcome the striving pilgrim, taking him by the hand. Such scenes may have been further influenced by a passage in the *Discourses* of St. Symeon the New Theologian (942–1022): "Thus as we ascend the ladder by one step after another we shall arrive, as well I know, to the very city of heaven. There . . . our Master stands and peers out, saying to us all, 'Come to me, all who labor and are heavy-laden, and I will give you rest.' When we have arrived there we shall see Him as far as man is able so to do, and receive at His hands the kingdom of Heaven."[168] Or as Wu Li's precise contemporary Thomas Traherne (1637–1674) puts it: "The Cross of Christ is the Jacob's ladder by which we Ascend into the Highest Heavens."[169] In juxtaposing the Cross with the ladder to the gates of Heaven in his poem, Wu Li is therefore orchestrating ancient Christian imagery in classical Chinese verse, employing suitable terms from the *Ch'u tz'u* where they are useful and newly coined terms (*shih tzu* 十字, "Cross") where no Chinese precedent exists.

One last possible source for the ladder image in this poem must be mentioned: The façade of St. Paul's in Macao still stands,[170] and on the second tier from the top can be seen relief carvings of the instruments of the Passion flanked by angels, including the Cross itself, the nails, the hammer, the crown of thorns—and the ladder, clearly depicted in frontal position with its nine rungs. Wu Li would have seen it many times during his stay in Macao.

The fifth poem of the sequence, "Singing of the Source and Course of Holy Church," is of particular interest for the light it throws on Wu Li's response to the Jesuit claim that the Chinese classics contain references to the God of Abraham and Jacob:

> I used to chant that poem of Chou
>     about "ascending and descending":
> it was like clouds or fog dispersing,
>     so I could see the azure sky.
> I never suspected a world of brilliance
>     double that of sun and moon
> would start with the year *keng-shen*
>     of the *Yüan-shou* reign.
> Learning then had new knowledge
>     with blessings pure imbued;
> the Way attained far-reaching care,
>     the holy work complete.
> I wish to follow cloud-pendants of jade
>     to hear exalted singing;
> how could the pearl of the black dragon alone
>     serve to illuminate that poem? [?]

One of the prime exhibits, so to speak, in the Jesuit case was poem 235, *Wen Wang* 文王, the first poem in the *Ta ya* 大雅 section of the *Shih ching* 詩經.[171] The first stanza of this important poem begins, "*Wen Wang tsai shang, yü chao yü t'ien*" 文王在上, 於昭于天; and it ends, "*Wen Wang chih chiang, tsai ti tso yu*" 文王陟降, 在帝左右. These lines Karlgren translates, "Wen Wang is on high, / oh he shines in heaven; . . . Wen Wang ascends and descends, / he is on the left and right of God." Waley translates the first two lines identically, and the last two he renders: "King Wen ascends and descends / On God's left hand, on His right."[172] This is one of the passages, as we have seen, which caused trouble to Chu Hsi and other Neo-Confucian thinkers who wished to interpret *t'ien* and *ti* as mere metaphors for *li*, "principle." We expect Wu Li to present the passage as a foreshadowing or glimmering of God's presence, in accordance with the Jesuit interpretation, and indeed he tells us that he was inspired by it to a sense of something beyond. But the rhetorical structure of the lines surprisingly seems to lend a different nuance to Wu's interpretation: He tells us he "used" (*ts'eng* 曾) to chant the poem; but when he learned of the Incarnation (which he dates to the year *keng-shen* 庚申 of the *Yüan-shou* reign—strictly speaking, 1 B.C.), he was *surprised*; he "never suspected" (*pu t'u* 不圖) that the true brilliance of God would come to earth. The unexpectedness is reinforced by his further use of the particle *ch'üeh* 卻: "contrary to expectation." In other words, the implication is that for Wu Li the passage about Wen Wang was less a foreshadowing than a false lead. Just as poem 11 in the series, as we have seen, takes pains to distinguish the Trinity from the "threeness" of Confucian cosmology, this one seems to emphasize that the only true *descent* of God would be the historical Incarnation, not the descent of Wen Wang (in Karlgren's words) "when coming as a spirit, to accept sacrificial gifts."

The sixth poem of the series presses into service a Buddhist term and a famous image from Su Shih 蘇軾 (1037–1101) to emphasize the ephemerality of worldly affairs, but in an unmistakably Christian context:

> By nature I have always felt quite close to the Way;
> when done with chanting my new poems,
>     I always concentrate my spirit.
> Prior to death, who believes
>     in the joy of the land of Heaven?
> After the end, then comes amazement
>     at the truth of the fires of hell!
> The achievements and fame of this ephemeral world:
>     footprints of geese on snow;
> this body, this shell in a lifetime of toil:
>     dust beneath horses' hoofs.

And what is more, the flowing of time
    presses man so fast:
let us plan to ask carefully about the ford
    that leads to the true source.

The key line here is the fifth: "*fou-shih kung-ming hung chua hsüeh*" 浮世功名鴻爪雪. "*Fou-shih,*" "floating (ephemeral) world," is well known both as a Buddhist term and in its ironically this-worldly use as a description of the life and culture of the gay quarters in Tokugawa Japan. The "footprints of geese on snow" alludes to Su Shih's great poem, "Echoing Tzu-yu's Poem, Longing for the Past at Mien-ch'ih" 和子由澠池懷舊,[173] which opens with an extended four-line presentation of the metaphor in question:

Human life everywhere—would you know
    what it is like?
It must be likened to a flying goose
    alighting on muddy snow.
On the mud for a while his claw-prints do remain,
while the goose flies off—what way to reckon
    whether east or west? . . .

But the Christian turn is given this imagery in Wu Li's poem by the previous couplet: There is a "land of Heaven," a "true source" to which a "ford" does lead (last line); and there are "fires of hell" to be avoided. But few believe in their existence; only after death will these nonbelievers be surprised, some of them, unpleasantly. It is then that the "east or west" of the goose's destination will be "reckoned" after all.

The eighth poem in the series introduces the theme of the Trinity, which will be more fully developed in the eleventh poem.

In the very highest place, deep within a mansion
    dwells a family perfectly united, loving and devoted.
Beyond past, beyond present, the three Persons are one;
penetrating heaven, penetrating earth,
    the one family is three!
Those who are known as "daily improving"
    to praise the Spirit are worthy;

> the world possesses a wondrous flower
> > fit to protect the holy.
> On painted walls, year after year,
> > we contemplate their images:
> pure incense rises in orderly spirals
> > to where their noses inhale.

Wu's first presentation of one of Christianity's most difficult doctrines employs the metaphor of the family. The Trinity is like a perfectly united family—a single entity, but consisting of three persons. The images of Father, Son, and Spirit (perhaps in the form of a dove) are depicted in wall paintings and venerated with incense.

The ninth poem of the sequence orchestrates imagery drawn mostly from the fourth chapter of Revelation, the scene in which the four-and-twenty elders bow down before the throne of God as they hear the angelic hymn "Holy, Holy, Holy (Lord God Almighty)"—first heard by Isaiah as sung by the seraphim (Isaiah 6:2–3):

> In glory they are crowned in jade,
> > and clothed in robes of gold;
> their merit earned in bloody battle,
> > childlike their hearts.
> A valley of ten thousand colors,
> > fragrances and flowers;
> a forest from a single root,
> > a single trunk and vine.
> To soul's repletion, intoxicated
> > they drink from the cup of Jesus;
> with dancing limbs, they stretch forward to listen
> > to the harp of David.
> "Holy, Holy, Holy," their voices ceaselessly cry:
> beneath the throne of the Lamb
> > echoes the sound of their song.

In addition to the imagery derived from Revelation, Wu Li has woven into this poem imagery of King David and his harp, the Jesse Tree ("a forest from a single root"), and the Eucharist ("they drink from the cup of Jesus"). The repeated *sheng* 聖, "Holy," is brilliantly and unexpectedly worked into the penultimate seven-character line: *sheng-sheng-sheng sheng hu-pu-tuan* 聖聖聖聲呼不斷, and the whole succeeds in conveying the sense of ecstatic joy and visionary exaltation that are so characteristic of Christianity—and rare if not nonexistent in traditional Chinese poetry.

The theme of the Eucharist is fully developed in poem 10:

> Utterly transcendent, His wondrous essence
> > was never limited to place;
> to bring life to the teeming people
> > He showed Himself, then hid.
> Effortlessly, a single standard—
> > a new cake baked for us;
> as before, the six directions have one supreme Lord.
> In the human realm, now we have
> > a whole burnt offering;
> in Heaven for eternity is preserved our daily bread.
> I have incurred so many transgressions,
> > yet am allowed to draw near:
> with body and soul fully sated,
> > tears moisten my robe.

The "new cake baked for us" is none other than God, and the "six directions" have this "one supreme Lord"—the very situation Ch'ü Yu-chung, in his petition to Yellow Heaven, could only wish for. And the human realm and heavenly realm are now linked. Spirit has taken on flesh; "daily bread" is preserved in Heaven yet available on earth, the new burnt offering—God does not delight in ordinary burnt offerings (Psalms 51:16–19)—which is both a gift offered to God and received from God, and actually God Himself. The poem ends as a prayer of preparation for holy communion—the poet grateful that he is allowed to approach the chalice even though unworthy, a fundamental theme of early prayers of preparation for communion by Church fathers such as St. Basil the Great (ca. 330–379)—and a prayer of thanksgiving *after* communion: "tears" (of joyful thanksgiving) "moisten my robe."

As a whole, "Singing of the Source and Course of Holy Church" succeeds in achieving Wu Li's goal of creating a Chinese Christian poetry, true to Chinese traditions of allusion, parallelism, and other familiar poetic techniques and true also to orthodox Christian theology, piety, and liturgical solemnity. Following "Singing of the Source of Holy Church" is another sequence of seven poems apparently based on the *Ch'i k'o* 七克, "Seven Overcomings," written by Fr. Diego de Pantoja "in collaboration with Xu Guangqi," as Gernet puts it,[174] and published in 1614. This book, which Gernet says "contains practical advice for the struggle against the seven deadly sins," also bore a preface by another pillar of the Chinese church, Yang T'ing-yün. The idea of "overcoming the self," *k'o chi* 克己, formed part of the Confucian conception of self-cultivation and was introduced in the *Analects* 12.1. In the translation of D. C. Lau, the key passage reads: "The Master said, 'To return to the observance of the rites through overcoming the self constitutes benevolence'" (*k'o chi fu li wei jen* 克己復禮為仁).[175] This is the familiar Stoic claim that the self can be overcome by the self; as Confucius goes on to say, "The practice of benevolence depends on oneself alone, and not on others" (*wei jen yu chi, erh yu jen hu tsai* 為仁由己而由人乎哉). He then further defines the practice of "overcoming the self" in these terms: "Do not look unless it is in accordance with the rites; do not listen (etc.); do not speak (etc.); do not move (etc.)." The seminal Neo-Confucian thinker Ch'eng I 程頤 (1033–1107) would stress this passage and develop it in his "Four Admonitions" (*Szu chen* 四箴) on proper "looking," "listening," "speaking," and "moving (acting),"[176] and these in turn would have an incalculable influence on seventeenth-century Ch'eng-Chu revivalists not only in China, but in Japan as well. Ishikawa Jōzan 石川丈山 (1583–1672)—close friend of Hayashi Razan 林羅山 (1583–1657), the chief Confucian advisor to the early Tokugawa shoguns—wrote out the complete text of these admonitions in four different styles of calligraphy, one for each admonition.[177] Wu Li would certainly have been familiar with the "Admonitions" and the *Analects* passage from which they derived.

But in his *Ch'i-k'o* poems,[178] Wu Li turns to the Christian perspective and devotes one poem to each of the Seven Deadly Sins:

pride (*ao* 傲); avarice (*lin* 吝; the term *t'an* 貪 is used in the poem itself); lust (*yin* 淫); anger (*fen* 忿); envy (*tu* 妬); gluttony (*t'ao* 饕); and sloth (*tai* 怠). In placing pride first, Wu is in accordance with the ancient theological position that pride is the supreme and truly original sin from which the others ultimately derive. Eve eats of the forbidden fruit when the serpent promises, "Ye shall be as gods, knowing good and evil" (Genesis 3:5–6). The real temptation here is not so much the lust of popular theology as it is the Faustian urge to achieve total knowledge: to become a deity. One of the earliest and most influential Christian writers on the deadly sins (of which he in fact identified eight), Evagrius Ponticus (345–399), wrote, "The demon of pride is the cause of the most damaging fall for the soul. For it induces the monk to deny that God is his helper and to consider that he himself is the cause of virtuous actions."[179] Following Evagrius, St. John Cassian (ca. 365–ca. 435) showed the connection between pride and humility: "I have won the grace of humility and simplicity. With contrite spirit I have laid off the yoke of pride. . . . [But] if I am not to suffer a more grievous wound as a consequence of my victory I must use all my strength to say aloud, 'Come to my help, O God; Lord, hurry to my rescue.'"[180] These passages clarify the crucial distinction between the Christian and Confucian concepts: The individual is *not* "himself. . . the cause of virtuous actions" (Evagrius), but rather has overcome by winning God's "grace of humility" (Cassian). From such a perspective, the Confucian (or Stoic) who claims to have overcome the faults of the self by the self alone is actually guilty of pride. This Wu Li must have understood when he wrote his own poetic treatment of the subject:

> Overcoming Pride
>
> The evil of pride—would you know what it is like?
> An arrogant lion, untamable!
> With strong heart he boasts of what he possesses;
> looks down around as if there were no one else.
> For a few days he pierces the clouds on high,
> then falls to the dust for a thousand autumns.
> How diligently to overcome this in oneself?
> Of ten thousand virtues, one—humility—rings true.

The culmination of Wu Li's extraordinary experiment—the creation of an authentically Chinese Christian poetry—came with his decision to write such poems not in the *shih* form, but rather in the form of suites of *ch'ü* 曲 poems. The manuscript of his poems of this type, entitled "Compendium of Orthodox Sounds of Heavenly Music," was recovered, as we have seen, by Fang Hao in 1946 from the Zikawei library. The book appears never to have been printed until 1950, when Fang Hao was able to produce a punctuated version with the names of the various *ch'ü* modes and tunes (omitted in the manuscript) provided and with annotations. Unfamiliar with the arcane branch of Chinese literature studies that specializes in *ch'ü* prosody, Fang solicited the help first of Lu Ch'ien 盧前 and then later of Cheng Ch'ien. Without the pioneering work of these scholars, the poems would be even more difficult to read than they are, as they must be considered among the most completely original poems in all of Chinese literature, owing relatively little in their diction to earlier Chinese poetry, unlike even such *shih* poems as the sequence "Singing of the Source and Course of Holy Church," which borrows numerous phrases from the *Ch'u tz'u* and other Chinese classics for a Christian purpose.

The first suite consists of a series of poems describing the Mass, with particular emphasis on the movements and utterances of the officiating priest. Fang Hao has shown that certain of the phrases are based on a contemporary liturgical manual and has annotated the appropriate passages.[181] As an example of these poems, I offer this translation of a poem to the tune *Tung-ou ling* 東甌令:

Again he washes his hands,
and then turns around.
He prays that he and all assembled sinners
may be washed clean with no iota left:
only then may they not betray
Jesus's compassion.
And why does he make the sign of the Cross
    over and over again?
The holy death took place nailed thereon.[182]

Other poems present episodes from Christ's life and passion or even sweeping overviews of God's entire economy. One poem from the suite, "Music of Harmonious Heaven in Reverent Thanks to the Lord of Heaven" 敬謝天主鈞天樂[183] (a title which assimilates to the Christian Heaven the "Harmonious Heaven" of Lieh Tzu's anecdote, familiar by now, about King Mu of Ch'in's dream journey—also used in Ch'ü Yu-chung's poem about "Yellow Heaven"), combines the Incarnation (there is specific reference to the Virgin Birth) with the Presentation in the Temple. The names of Joseph (Jo-se 若瑟) and Simeon (Hsi-mo-ang 西默盎) are rendered in transliteration:

> —To the tune, *Hsi ch'ien ying* 喜遷鶯
>
> Late in Han
> God's Son came down from Heaven
> to save us people
> and turn us towards the good.
> His grace goes wide!
> Taking flesh through the virginity
>     of the Holy Mother in a stable He was born.
> Joseph too came to present Him in the temple:
> there to offer praise was
> Simeon.
> They say He can
> save our souls from their destructiveness
> and sweep away the devil's wantonness.

In two other poems, one from "Musical Stanzas to Admonish the Proud" (*ching ao yüeh-chang* 警傲樂章) and one from "On Rules and Statutes" (*yung kuei-ch'eng* 咏規程), the Incarnation is placed in the context of the Fall:[184]

> —To the tune, *Sheep on the Mountain Slope*
>
> Men in a dream,
> unhumble, unforgiving;
> bodies in illness,
> undoctored and uncured.

The heaven in our nature
we let wither away;
our souls in fallen state,
faded—where are they now?
But the Lord came down from Heaven
to show His grace in the distant West,
removing the sins of the world,
the sins of the world from the beginning washed away.
And feeling compassion on us all,
to save and take our souls!
But Oh
we living creatures still cling to delusion,
truly insane!
We are the devil's slaves
all unawares.

  —To the tunes, *Music for the Spring* and *Victorious Music*
I have heard the heavenly country
was our native land.
First evil born with
Eve and Adam:
how could they lack this ill?
Crossing Heaven, gleaning sin—who could pull them back?
And so all souls
did evil, deserved punishment.
It moved the One Lord,
but His mercy then was hard to count upon!

Therefore Jesus
came down and was born,
came down to save us and redeem
ten thousand countries, distant places.

The doctrine of Adam and Eve, one of the aspects of Western learning rejected by the diarist Lu Lung-chi, is here asserted with full orthodoxy. Wu Li demonstrates in this poem his understanding of the redemptive relationship between the Fall and the Incarnation; he even changes tune patterns to signal the new dispensation—from "Music for the Spring" (*i ch'un yüeh* 宜春樂) to "Victorious Music" (*ta sheng yüeh* 大勝樂). We may even go so far as to suggest that Wu Li intended the allusion to "victory" in the title of the second tune pattern, even though such titles usually bear no relationship to the actual content of the poem. In this case, the "victory" would be the supreme victory of redemption through the Incarnation. The first of these two poems states that the Incarnation took place in the "distant West" (*t'ai-hsi* 泰西), while the second asserts that the redemption of all nations (*wan kuo* 萬國), however distant from ancient Judea, was intended.

The *ch'ü* form was originally associated with drama, and perhaps most remarkable of all in this generally remarkable set of poems is the series "Moses Admonishes the People—Musical Stanzas" (*Mei-se yü chung yüeh chang* 每瑟諭衆樂章),[185] which bears this subtitle: "When Moses was done with his final testament, he continued in song and admonished the people, saying . . ." Here Wu Li can be said to have created a dramatic monologue for Moses; it is difficult to conceive of any more bizarre phenomenon in literary history than an imaginary oration by Moses intoned in classical Chinese, and yet that is what Wu Li gives us in these poems. In one of them,[186] Moses reminds the people that there is only one Lord of Heaven (the very proposal put before Yellow Heaven almost in desperation by Ch'ü Yu-chung but believed actually to be the case in Judaism and Christianity), describes for them the land of Canaan which he himself will never enter, and berates them for rebelling against God:

This wilderness!
If only you, His people,
      acknowledge one Lord of Heaven—
there is no second one!—
the Lord of Heaven will confer that rich and fertile land
to care for and to cultivate.

That land is luxuriant, fruitful,
      impossible to match!

The five grains profusely grow,
　　　there are no weeds and tares;
and it is even richer
in tender kid, fine wine.

Milk and honey, meat and oil, there do overflow!

The Lord of Heaven loves you as His children:

who could foresee that you, once full and sated,
　　　would act like animals,

kicking, biting back!

—forgetting His great gift.

In striving toward the full prophetic voice in Chinese poetry, Wu Li is perhaps attempting the impossible. Is this a fascinating but ultimately failed experiment lacking either precedent or later influence? Or is it a major achievement that throws new light on the potential creativity of later Chinese poetry?

The "Compendium of Orthodox Sounds of Heavenly Music" earned the praise of *ch'ü* scholar Cheng Ch'ien, who helped Fang Hao prepare the difficult manuscript for publication. In a colophon to the book, he comments:

> In reading this work, I have found the metrical patterns to be perfectly arranged, and the key tunes to be thoroughly masterful. Moreover [the poems] are utterly elegant, profound and beautiful. Their tones are sparse, the flavor "bland": indeed he has opened new territory in southern and northern *ch'ü*. Thus we realize that when it comes to the talents of a gifted man, there is truly no task to which they will be unsuccessfully applied.[187]

In describing the flavor of these poems as "bland" (*tan*), Cheng is paying the same paradoxical compliment to Wu Li that Wu Chih-chen had paid to Sung Wan, employing a key term of Sung poetic aesthetics.

Cheng goes on to argue that because of Wu Li's greater familiarity with southern culture, his tune patterns from southern and central China have perfectly matched rhymes, while his "northern sets" are not always perfect in this way. He then makes this important point:

Ch'ü. . . are not suited to the explication of principle [that is, discursive diction], but the works in this book lodge feeling in principle—they are serious and earnest. Reading them is like being in the presence of an elder of great virtue who "takes your ear and exhorts you to your face." Could a man whose nurturement in learning was not profound and solid, and whose artistry was not in accord with the Way, have achieved this?

Cheng also develops a brilliant comparison with certain anonymous *ch'ü* of the Yüan dynasty collected in a book entitled *Tzu-jan chi* 自然集, "Anthology of the Self-So," and entirely based on Taoist alchemy. He describes them as being little better than doggerel prescriptions in rhyme for Taoist elixirs, filled with technical terminology and "fit only to put you to sleep." "If we compare them with these poems of Yü-shan, they are so far removed that it cannot be calculated in mere miles."

Cheng believes that Wu Li has succeeded where others have failed in employing *ch'ü* for religious poetry. "I always enjoy reading the poems of Wu Li," writes Fr. Albert Chan, S.J., "especially his religious poems: so artistic and so full of devotion."[188]

*Illustrations*

Plate 1. *Auspicious Fungus Growing at the Ts'en-wei-chü Residence,* 1659. Hanging scroll, ink and color on paper. 49¾ × 23¾ in. Kyoto National Museum. The painting has five inscriptions: two by the artist himself, dated 1659 *(bottom right of upper portion)* and 1661 *(upper left);* one by Ch'ien Ch'ien-i dated 1660 *(upper right);* one by Wu Wei-yeh, undated *(upper center);* and one by the poet, painter, and seal carver, Yen Shih dated 1661 *(bottom left).*

Plate 2. *Whiling Away the Summer at the Inkwell Thatched Hall*, 1679. Handscroll, ink on paper. 14⁵/₁₆ × 105⁵/₈ in. Detail. The Metropolitan Museum of Art, New York, Purchase, Douglas Dillon Gift, 1977.81.

Plate 3. *Pine Wind from Myriad Valleys,* un-dated; "Probably executed towards the end of his life" (Henry Kleinhenz). Hanging scroll, ink and color on paper. $43^{1}/_{8} \times 10^{3}/_{16}$ in. The Cleveland Museum of Art, John L. Severance Fund, 54.584.

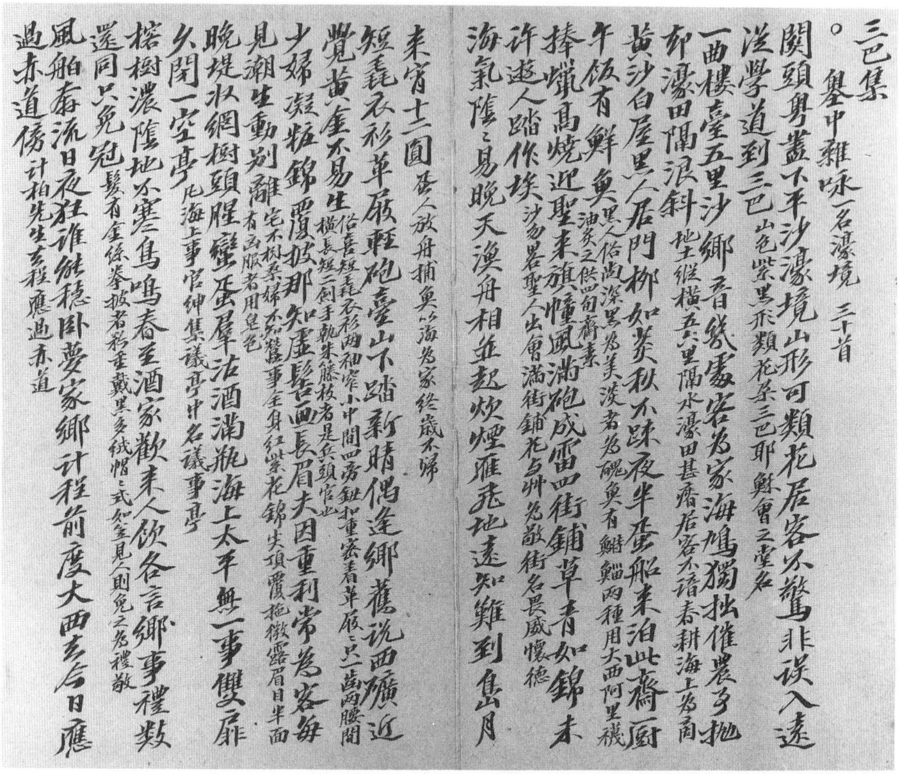

三巴集

奥中雜咏一名濠境　三十首

関頭舉盡下平沙濠境山形可類花屋客不驚非誤入逺
滋學道到三巴山岩紫黑飛類花莖三巴耶鮮曾三塞名

一西樓臺五里沙郷音發處客為家海舶獨抵催農多抛
郤濠田偶浪斜黄沙白屋里人居門柳如葵秋不斷夜半牽舡来泊此喬廚
坐繞檐五里開水濠田甚齋岩客不語春耕海上名西禢

午伍有鮮魚

捧觴高燒迎聖来旗幢風滿砲成雷四街舖草青如錦未
許逺人踏作埃沙巴曾滿街舖花名街盛懷德

海氣陰之易晚天溟舟相並起炊煙雁落地逺知難到焦山月

右肖十二圓

短蓑不衫草廠輕砲臺山下踏新晴偶逢郷舊說西嬪近
覺黄金不易生

少婦凝粧錦霞披那突虛髻画長眉大因重利常為客毎

見朝生動別離

晚堤松網樹頭腥羶臿屠拏法酒満瓶海上太平無一事雙扉
久聞一空亭

榕樹濃陰地不寒烏鳴春至酒家歡未人飲各言郷事禮數
遷同只免宽

風舶春流日夜狂誰能穩臥夢家郷計程前度大西来后日應
過赤道傍計柏先生玄程應過赤道

Plate 4. Poems by Wu Li in his own calligraphy: *San-pa chi, Miscellaneous Poems on Macao*. Album, ink on paper. Each leaf 8.86 × 10.63 in. Detail: first two leaves, showing title and first ten poems. Hong Kong Museum of Art, by permission of the Urban Council of Hong Kong.

# The Poems

# Poems on
# Traditional Themes

## *No Direction—Following Rhymes*

For ten years, my steps like duckweed
      have had no real direction;
"grievously weeping at West Terrace,"
      the tears have not yet dried.

Everywhere is desolate wasteland,
      covered with new houses;

how many left to feel sadness at old robes and caps?

Along the river, as spring departs,
      there is poetic feeling;

beyond the frontier, where wild geese fly,
      snowy atmosphere is cold.

Today the dust of wartime
      has still not settled down;

with whom will I get drunk and grow old
      holding fishing rods?

MCC, 2/17a. Hsieh Ao 謝翱 (1249–1295), upon the death of Wen
T'ien-hsiang 文天祥 (1236–1283), established a shrine to Wen at West Terrace and wrote an essay called *A Record of Grievously Weeping at West Terrace*
西臺慟哭記.

## Autumn Night

Autumn night—sleep will not take hold;
autumn sounds are filling my ears.
The wind blows loud, drowning drums and horns;
the moon is small, darkening the mountain town.
Weeping in wilderness—how can it be stopped?
The war goes on, still there is no peace.
My friends—where do they lodge tonight?
Tears of frustration criss-cross my face.

MCC, 2/17a.


## The Sick Horse

His coat, his bone, still finer than the herd,
but deep in autumn, illness hits him hard.
Battlefield deserted, but for green of grass,
the warrior can only sadly sing.
Strength worn out, dust without an end:
a fading whinny—how many years are left?
His master's kindness, we are sure, must not be super-
    ficial:
tears of blood beneath clear skies are scattered on the
    sedge.

MCC, 2/17a–b.

## *Escaping to Water Country*

For two years now I've grieved my fate
        is like a floating plant;
my temple hairs before my eyes
        have gradually turned gray.
In my old village to lament the autumn
        only crickets are left,
while here on foreign land, sadness at rain
        I share with the night herons.
In the south, I've heard it said,
        barbarian horses are received;
in the capital, they claim,
        they've pulled down the banners of Han!
How could we have at such a time cessation of the war?
I'd go back home where I'd be greeted
        by a streamful of yellow leaves.

MCC, 2/17b.

## *Lamenting for a Friend*

The cassia branch you never won—
    I know you harbored resentment;
your poetry manuscript alone remains—
    with tearful eyes I read it.
Moss in the courtyard still retains
    footprints where you walked;
autumn fireflies are stymied—the books
    they illuminated for you
        now lie scattered about.
Ailanthus stand by the crumbling hut,
    chanting chilly in the wind;
geese roost on the desolate embankment,
    fearful of cold rain.
I look back after hanging my solitary sword:
the white poplars sigh and sough,
    the road goes on and on.

MCC, 2/18b. "Cassia branch": a metaphor for the coveted *chin-shih* degree. "Fireflies . . . illuminated": an allusion to a certain Ch'e Yin 車胤 (d. ca. 397), a diligent but impoverished student who could not afford lamp oil and hence studied by the light of fireflies. "Hanging . . . sword": An allusion to the story of a Mr. Chi-tzu and a Mr. Hsü. Mr. Hsü admired Chi-tzu's sword, but never openly asked for it. Upon his death, Chi-tzu hung the sword on one of the trees beside his grave. The story is attributed to Liu Hsiang 劉向 (77–6 B.C.) in the notes to a letter by Liu Chün 劉峻 (462–521) in the *Wen hsüan*, ch. 43, p. 954.

## On a Spring Day the "Traveler Through Mist," Master Wang, Invited Me to Visit His West Field Estate

This famous garden is deeply hidden
  within the green shade;
a little pavilion among clearing clouds
  reached by a narrow path.
Along stone railings, birds shake off
  the flower-dew, so white;
in water-sky, fishermen sing
  as setting sun turns red.
We open bamboo blinds—far mountains
  limitless in spring;
trembling the walls, misty waves—
  moonlight fills the air.
With cups of wine and mouth-organ songs
  we come to share enjoyment;
inspecting old books, looking at paintings—
  what end to inspiration?

MCC, 2/18b. "West Field Estate" was the garden estate of Wu Li's master in painting, Wang Shih-min (1592–1680). In the third line, "railings" is a tentative conjecture for a one-character hiatus in the original text.

## At Wu-hsing on a Moonlit Night, Thinking of Home

The wind is strong, the crumbling house
    deep among creepers and vines;
fledgling swallows have deserted the rafters,
    moonlight floods the door.
Beyond bamboo, glittering lake-light
    links the wilds with white;
above the wall, mountain colors
    face the gateway, green.
From afar I yearn for my young son,
    his craziness hard to cure!
I've still not learned why the traveler's hair
    so easily turns to gray.
Flowers fall; after sobering up
    from drinking Wu-ch'eng wine
what man would not now call to mind
    the garden pavilion back home?

MCC, 2/18b–19a.

## At Hsiang-ch'eng Lake, Yearning for the Past

The rippling waves cling to the sky,
>way out, there's no horizon;

where sweet-voiced orioles are singing,
>just two or three houses stand.

Along the stream lined with green willows
>are many fishermen;

before the gate of sumac trees
>all the flowers have fallen.

The reedy bank parts in the middle
>revealing distant peaks;

the bamboo bridge turns to the west,
>by ragged clouds obscured.

How sad, these places made famous by great men—
>along the entire route

are delicate grass and desolate mist,
>and now the sun goes down.

MCC, 2/19a.

## *Untying the Hawser*

I moor my solitary cabin—
    and sunset comes again;
where green ripples are touched by red
    all is in a haze.
Old friends in poetry
    age with autumn's passing;
hometown mountains in my dreams
    grow barren after rain.
Wind stifles cries of wild geese
    as they fly in pairs;
clouds hang low over forest colors,
    darkening their expanse.
The stream ahead is desolate,
    few "water lilies" or "perch":
this "Chang Han" now leads a life
    that easily turns to pain.

---

MCC, 2/19b–20a. Chang Han (early 4th century) was an official who grew so homesick for the "water-lily soup" and "sliced perch" of his hometown that he left his official position and returned home. It was when the autumn winds blew that he felt the longing for these delicacies. See Richard B. Mather, ed. and trans., *Shih-shuo hsin-yü*: A New Account of Tales of the World (Minneapolis: University of Minnesota Press, 1976), pp. 201 and 500.

## *After the Troops Have Withdrawn,*
## *En Route to Nan-yang*

The woods are empty—only setting sun;
the place remote—few signs of lingering spring.
I want to find out how to reach Nan-yang,
but in the next village, nobody is left.

MCC, 2/20a.


## *Stopped by Ice*

On the cold canal a full ten days,
　　　sails and masts are frozen;
in morning snow, a thousand houses,
　　　hearth-smoke rising slow.
Why is it that the news of spring
　　　this year must come so late?
Along Sui-dynasty embankments
　　　no willow catkins yet!

MCC, 2/20a.

## *Traveling at Dawn*

I leave at dawn, chanting poems
      along the River Huai;
a few establishments—thatched inns
      have single lamps hung out.

Roosters crow as snow clears up,
      the moon sinks in the sand;
geese fly over high-piled ice,
      light soon fills the sky!

Houses too few to form a village,
      woods completely still;
not one traveler in view,
      road stretching on and on.

All I pass is territory
      once held by Marquis Han;
only fishing wharfs appear
      before my horse's head.

MCC, 2/20a–b.

## On an Autumn Day Together with Censor Hsü Ch'ing-yü Visiting Yao Peak

Yao Peak, in sounds of bell and gong;
one path piercing cloudy woods.
Yellow leaves—the poet's inspiration;
quiet mountain—the old monk's mind.
Tea and mulberry, tranquil autumn bank;
duck and egret, darkened river sky.
Hsieh's clogs make us forget how steep it is:
mist and cloud around this place lie thick.

MCC, 2/20b.


## Inscribed on a Painting, *Inquiring After Plum Blossoms*

Meandering, by stream and forest
      he passes the terrace of stone;
fragrant breezes all along the road,
      moon hovering above.
Done chanting his poem, he cries out
      for the guest of Solitary Mountain:
he wants to ask him, "Have the plums
      put forth their blossoms yet?"

MCC, 2/20b–21a. "Guest of Solitary Mountain": Lin Pu (967–1028), famous recluse who lived on Solitary Mountain at West Lake, with "plum blossoms as his wife and cranes as his children." He is the author of perhaps the most famous Chinese poem on the subject of plum blossoms.

## *Yangchou*

South and north once came together,
        meeting at this place;
that glory has diminished; how does it feel now?
People's houses still exist,
        in dreams of jeweled flowers;
but do not count on jars of wine
        and songs of moonlit nights!
Towers, pavilions high and low—
        beyond the bridges, few;
hoofs and wheels still come and go,
        against the setting sun.
And every year in disappointment
        spring winds blow again,
snapping off weeping willow branches
        into the old canals.

MCC, 2/21a.

## *Reply to Ts'an-wen*

Ts'an-wen came by to visit; when I returned home I found we had missed each other. Following the original rhymes of his poem, I respond to him with a disclaimer:

All night the west wind shook the emerald woods;

the old mountain has never betrayed
> my desire to recline among the clouds.

This body of mine is only suited
> to live beyond lake and sky

where waters are broad and mist profuse—
> don't waste time searching for me!

MCC, 2/22a.


## *En Route to Nan-yang*

En route to Nan-yang I saw red lotus and green willows and composed this (the willows were hand-planted by the late Mr. Chu Mei-lu, Minister of Works):

Clusters of houses, tiny groupings
> along the western dike;

beyond the willows, a bridge leads on
> to turn after turn of road.

Here in the fragrance of white lotus-root
> a living can be made:

little boats cast little nets,
> large boats, massive seines.


MCC, 2/23a–b. "Mr. Chu Mei-lu": Chu Chih-hsi 朱之錫 (1624–1666), a respected official who in 1656 became director-general of Yellow River and Grand Canal Conservancy. According to E. S. Larsen, writing in Hummel, *Eminent Chinese of the Ch'ing Period* (p. 178), "He stressed the value of a ready supply of willow material for dike repairs, outlining a program of intensive cultivation of willow trees in the vicinity of threatened sections of the river."

## *After Traveling*

After traveling a long time, I became weary of the road, and the burning heat was intensely irritating. Suddenly I thought of a beautiful spot in Emei Mountain, like the one of which Shao-ling wrote: "How could I get to walk that layered ice with my bare feet!" My windowed cabin is half-full of brushes and ink-cakes, so I sketched roughly, mixing in something of Ying-ch'iu's and Tao-ning's methods, and came up with this:

Suddenly I thought of Emei Mountain—
> hot vapors cleared away!

Ten thousand peaks collecting snow,
> competing in craggy grandeur.

The light turned cold wants to descend
> to strengthen my poet's bones:

unexpected, cottony mist arises with the wind.

---

MCC, 2/23b. "Shao-ling": Tu Fu (712–770). "Ying-ch'iu" and "Tao-ning". Li Ch'eng (919–967) and Hsü Tao-ning (early 11th century), two great painters noted for their monumental landscapes. "Cottony mist": Possibly a reference to the mysterious phenomena associated with Emei Mountain in the writings of such Sung poets as Fan Ch'eng-ta (1126–1193) and Yang Wan-li (1127–1206). This poem was evidently inscribed on a painting by Wu himself.

The poem by Tu Fu cited by Wu Li is entitled "Suffering from the Heat in Early Autumn, as My Desk Continues to Be Piled High" (*Tu Shao-ling chi hsiang-chu*, ch. 6, p. 121). A commentator on Tu Fu's poetry named Chu Han 朱瀚 expressed doubt as to the authenticity of this poem, claiming that "there is not one line in the entire poem worth accepting." Apparently Wu Li thought otherwise. (The poem is dated 758 by the editors, when Tu was in Hua-chou in the north, not in Szechwan.)

## Inscribed on the Painting
*Crossing the Autumn River at Evening*

Deserted river, geese write "man"
    across the autumn sky;
rustic ferry, setting sunlight
    fills the ferry boat.
South and north, coming and going,
    without any end . . .
white duckweed and red smartweed
    stretching on and on.

MCC, 2/24a. The Chinese word for "man" (or "person") is written in a shape roughly like an inverted V; hence the V-shape formed by a flock of geese as they fly across the sky is often compared to the word for "man" and conjures up thoughts of an absent friend.

### *Studying the* Ch'in

I realize that since I started studying the *ch'in* zither together with Mr. Chi T'ien-chu beneath the gate of Master Ch'en Shan-min, over twenty years have passed unnoticed. I wanted to do a painting, *Singing Ch'in in the Pine Valley*, to convey my feelings, but I have been hampered by insufficient leisure. Now that I have returned north, I take my brush and do the painting without worrying about skill or clumsiness.

We studied *ch'in*, mysterious resonance
    brought to a crisp roundness;
the suffering I shared with you
    for over twenty years.
Today I lean against a pine
    listening to the waterfall:
This "tall mountain and flowing water"
    has never required strings!

MCC, 2/24a–b. "Tall Mountain and Flowing Water" is the name of the most famous *ch'in* composition, attributed to the legendary *ch'in* master Po Ya.

## *Suffering from the Rain*

The rainfall sounds heavier and heavier,
so mournful it will turn my hair all white!
Throughout the twin lakes, unfair to poor houses,
striking four walls with crashing waves.
Night, I dream I'm suspended in a boat;
dawn, I light the stove as rain seeps through my raincoat.
Above my bed there are many spots that leak;
the almanac says a Bad Luck Day draws near.

MCC, 2/24b–25a.

## *Echoing Chiang Nan-yai's Poem on the Cold Moon*

The winter moon is still worth viewing:
but what's the poet to do about the cold?
That pure radiance is like a lingering mirror,
but at year's end few look at it.
The chill irradiates field upon field to white;
the brightness strips each leaf from every tree.
Before descent it follows the snowy oar;
not yet full, pursues the chanter's saddle.
Gazing up, I remember autumn partings;
unable to sleep, grieve as night drags on.
At such a time I blow on frozen brush:
to catch that image in a painting will be hard.

MCC, 2/25a.

## *Lamenting for Master Wang Yen-k'o*
(Four Poems from a Group of Eight)

### 1

The news came from Lou River—I doubted, I
      believed . . .
By rainy window lamplight darkened,
      tears flowed into streams.
I called my boy—quickly, open up
      my bamboo trunk:
fish out all the poems he wrote me
      when he was alive.

### 2

I shouldered my book-box, on and on,
      following you through years;
at the ink-pond, your reflection
      hovers vaguely in the green.
Recall the start—together we copied
      the brush of Crazy Huang;
the colors of his rivers, features of his mountains,
      carefully discussed.

4

The place of pure seclusion towers high
  against the evening sky;
*wu-t'ung* blossoms have opened, the moon
  is void and full.

Its light trembles on four walls
  where your antique pictures hang:
as before, Hua-t'ing's paintings
  hang across from them.

*Poet's note:* On his walls are authentic works of the Sung and Yüan
dynasties; these he would always hang facing works by Hua-t'ing.

5

The days of your illness we grieved at downpours
  that never seemed to end;
now the corners of your eaves have fewer cooing doves.

Yet here in Black Robe Alley not a single spot is dry

because the tears of your sons and grandsons
  now are flowing through.

MCC, 2/26b–28a. Master Wang Yen-k'o: Wang Shih-min (1592–
1680), Wu Li's painting teacher. Crazy Huang: Huang Kung-wang (1269–
1354), one of the Four Masters of Yüan painting and a primary influence on
both Wang Shih-min and Wu Li. Hua-t'ing: Tung Ch'i-ch'ang (1555–1636),
the chief painter and painting theoretician of the late Ming dynasty.

## At the Stream Mouth

Since I moved here to live at the stream mouth,
though I'm not yet old, my hair's already white.
Every year we suffer from spring rains,
this year more torrential than before!
This old house has completely collapsed;
the waters block us from any human voice.
On all four sides no sign of kitchen fires;
just moist clouds darkening the colors of the trees.
On my little bed, a frog squats and croaks;
in our broken stove, a turtle hides its nest.
Few hamlets here have managed to survive;
how can we get shelter, rest, and food?
And who can we depend on to tell our sovereign,
our sovereign's door, behind nine lofty thresholds?

MCC, 2/28a–b.


## Seeing Off a Friend
(One Poem from a Set of Two)

Your journeying sail moves out to sea—
      far out there's no horizon;
I see only an endless sky, no speck of dust at all.
One day of windswept waves will bring
      twelve dangers to the ship:
please guard well your wandering body
      so it may return.

MCC, 2/28b.

## *Sent to Hanlin Compiler Mei-ts'un*

Water meanders, the stream turns back,
        the rocky road goes deep;
white clouds veil the house from view,
        trees give plenteous shade.
In the mountains you need not worry
        that neighing steeds may visit:
all you hear, the waterfall,
        clearing the wanderer's mind.

MCC, 2/28b–29a. Hanlin Compiler Mei-ts'un: Wu Wei-yeh (1609–1672), one of the greatest poets of the Ch'ing dynasty.

## *Echoing a Poem, "At a Buddhist Temple, at Leisure, Recording Things Experienced"*

Frost falls in a thousand woods,
        wild geese fill the sky:
a traveler's heart—lonely, cut off,
        his feelings the same as these.
The pond now shows no plants of spring—
        poems are hard to write.
The folding screen has autumn flies;
        paintings turn out bad.
Mountain masses, craggy, thrusting
        past the silkworm shed;
wavelets' brilliance, turning, winding
        through the garden of cranes.
From ancient times fine wine has beaten
        seeking discs of jade:
let me get drunk on T'iao-ch'i Stream,
        become a fisherman!

MCC, 2/29a.

## Echoing a Poem, "Planning to Buy Mountain Land Along the T'iao-ch'i Stream"

Recently I got to see the clouds above the lake;

happily I'd give my life to those woods and hills!

Listening to poems on moonlit nights—
    shared with skinny cranes;

buying wine in the village of flowers—
    riding my sturdy ox.

Green would fill new bamboo groves,
    bringing smiles of pride;

red would mark the field fires
    as I'd roam and wander.

Long ago, Hsiang P'ing cast off the trammels of the world,

forever to follow Master Primal Truth
    as he fishes the jade-green flow.

MCC, 2/29a–b. Hsiang P'ing 向平 (or Hsiang Ch'ang 長) was a scholar of the *I ching* in the first half of the first century. After marrying off all his children, he went wandering among the Five Sacred Peaks. "Master Primal Truth" was Chang Chih-ho 張志和 (ca. 742  ca. 782), a scholar who became a hermit-fisherman.

## Visiting the Temple of the Heavenly Sage and Singing of Chao Sung-hsüeh's Wall Painting of the Hsiao and Hsiang Rivers

In inches of space a thousand mountains stand;
with rushing waters ten thousand gullies flow.
Rain darkens the forests far and near;
waves break wildly, waterbirds plunge and float.
There is bamboo, and yet a lingering grief;
no flowers, still the scene conveys a sadness.
Where can I find a scissor from Ping-chou
to snip myself half a river of autumn?

MCC 2/29b. Ch'en Hu (1613–1675) accompanied Wu on this trip and wrote a poem following his rhyme words (Ch'en 6/2a–b). Chao Sung-hsüeh: Chao Meng-fu 趙孟頫 (1254–1322), a leading calligrapher and painter of the Yüan dynasty; also a fine poet. None of his wall paintings are known to survive today.

## On an Autumn Day, Together with Master Ch'üeh-an and Tzu-chuang, Taking a Trip to Tao-ch'ang Mountain

### 1

We touch our oars to lake beneath clear sky;
green mountains slant along two shores.
Pine gates enclose deep mystery;
the pathway darkens beneath overhanging bamboo.
Only gazing into distance shows autumn at its best;
seeking a hidden temple, even wrong turnings are fine!
Among cloudy peaks, where is it at last?
The bells and gongs are coming from the mist.

### 2

All day we climb, enjoying the fine view;
a thousand peaks, uneven in their shapes.
Yellow blossoms on mountain paths are calm;
white birds land on water-reflected sky.
In this land of Buddha still they talk of tigers;
outside monks' windows, here too they raise chickens.
Wine-drunk, we put off our return;
on city battlements, soon the crows will caw.

MCC, 2/29b–30a. Master Ch'üeh-an: Ch'en Hu (1613–1675), Wu Li's teacher in Confucianism. "Tzu-chuang" is unidentified.

## *Echoing a Poem, "Climbing the Many-Treasured Pagoda at Cloudy Peak"*

Now let us follow the single path
    up to the highest peak;
the ancient pagoda is surrounded
    by tinted leaves all thick.

Autumn waters, green, rush on
    to distant lands of Wu;
evening clouds, all red, embrace
    the massive peaks of Yüeh.

At the ferry, winds so brisk
    they drown out fishermen's songs;
from the cave-mouth clouds fly off
    revealing tracks of cranes.

Twisting, twisting crystal stream:
    where is it flowing to?
Kitchen smoke from hidden houses
    tops the blue-green pines.

MCC, 2/30a. Wu Li's teacher, Ch'en Hu, accompanied him on this trip and wrote the poem Wu is here echoing. See Ch'en Hu, *Ch'üeh-an hsien-sheng shih-ch'ao*, 6/2b.

## *After Rain*

After rain on the Double Ninth
      the air is dark and damp;
alone I sit in my studio,
      hold knees to chest, and chant!
My little staff now has no need
      to add strength to my legs:
fine mountains in these poems I climb,
      and gaze out at the view.

MCC, 2/32b. The "Double Ninth" (ninth day of the ninth lunar month) was traditionally a time to climb mountains and enjoy the autumn scenery.

## *Min-yü—Master Chin—Sent a Gift of Lamb Shoulder, But My Mountain Boy Would Not Acknowledge Receipt and Turned It Back*

On this winter day who knocks
      at the gate in wind-blown snow?
This gift from afar bears feelings
      warmer than the spring.
But my mountain boy does not receive it,
      in fact he sends it back:
could he possibly fear that *this* lamb
      would trample our vegetable garden?

MCC, 2/33a.

## *The Swallows Are Here*

The place where it leaks above my bed
      has long since formed a hole;
but I'm too lazy to make a new roof—
      I stuff it with old thatch!
I laugh at myself for being inferior
      to this swallow pair:
year after year when spring arrives
      they build a brand-new nest!

MCC, 2/33a.


## *[Inscribed on a Painting]*

My hermit's life, entirely passed within a single boat!
I ask the world for nothing, I only love pure calm.
I cast far off through rivers and lakes
      so I can read in peace,
yet ears and eyes still feel hemmed in
      by all these verdant mountains.

(Tomioka, pl. 32)

## Inscribed on Paintings

### 1

Along the paths, willow colors dark and delicate;
I want to depict the feelings of parting,
  but tears obscure my eyes.
The springtime geese, alas, are now all flying
  to the north;
how can this wanderer tolerate
  his exile south of the river?

MCC, 2/35a.

### 2

The rainfall ends, across a vast sky
  a whiff of ocean air;
trees on trees to homes of monks,
  wild geese on sandbanks everywhere.
Wind goes whistling, whistling through pines,
  travelers are few:
clouds white, mountains green,
  a chilly painted screen.

*Poet's note:* On the sixth day of the ninth month of the year *wu-shen* [October 11, 1668], I was returning from P'i-ling to Mount Yü. In the midst of desolate wind and rain, I had the good fortune to stop for a sip of tea and the offering of incense. On the evening of the eighth day [October 13] it cleared up; in happiness, I painted this. Wu Li, with inscribed poem.

 From inscription on the handscroll in the Palace Museum, Taipei. The poem (with 水 instead of 海) is poem 2 of the *t'i-hua* sequence; MCC, 2/35a.

### 3

My poet's bones in cold weather
    especially seem to thrive:
over ten thousand mountains, flying snow
    fills the river sky!
If you don't know where best to look
    for feelings of poetry:
there, among plum blossoms,
    by their shadows in the moonlight.

### 4

Flowing waters leisurely pass west
    of the sacred peak;
how many layers of tinted trees
    beyond the cloudy stream?
A visitor comes and all day long chants poems
    beside the window:
the pines are calm, and at the gate
    not a single bird is singing.

MCC, 2/35a–b.

### 5

Spring winds along embankments,
    grass burgeoning in rows;
on distant mountains mists are floating,
    drizzling rains clear up.
Before the gates of white-thatched houses
    stand the tallow trees:
as evening sun sets, from them sound
    the songs of partridges.

### 6

Returned from a dream I gaze to the west
    where emerald hills are faint;
a whole river of setting sunlight;
    birds have stopped their flights.
I want to pluck these green and yellow
    leaves of lotus plants
to send you to make into a robe
    for resting in the clouds.

MCC, 2/35b–36a.

### 7

Sparse plantain trees and bamboo houses
    west and east of Jang River;
how many bends of misty peaks,
    tree colors all the same!
Eyes brimful of wine-intoxication,
    which way do I turn?
At sunset, off to pay a visit
    to the Old Man of Huan-hua Stream!

The Old Man: Tu Fu.

### 8

Bend upon bend of blue stream-water,
    delicate fragrant plants:
thatched houses, auspicious trees,
    a thousand clustered trunks.
White wispy clouds go trailing off,
    the mountains grow in green;
I sit here, loving to chant poems
    as autumn leaves start to yellow.

MCC, 2/36a.

### 9

Jade mountains where most beautiful
    are rows of lotus flowers:
just inches from Peach Blossom Spring,
    yet the road bends thousands of times.
I cannot tell if anyone will ever know this realm:
year after year, raining blossoms and white clouds
    seal it off.

### 10

A rainfall ends, tree colors freshen;
deep in the hall I sit alone, serene,
    no speck of dust.
No need to plan now anymore for trips
    on rivers and lakes:
a traveler comes visiting in autumn,
    bringing purple brasenia.

MCC, 2/36a–b.

11

The eastern gully divides and branches—
      a western gully flows;
the whole stream lined with red-leaf trees,
      at evening row on row.
Empty pavilion—for a while
      on rush mat I meditate:
the sun is escorting autumn sails
      where white gulls rise and go.

12

The twisting stream slants and branches
      past the willow embankment;
autumn leaves on distant hills—
      half are gosling yellow.
Who's that man with belly bared
      in the riverside pavilion,
serenely laughing at river clouds
      so busy bringing rain?

MCC, 2/36b–37a.

13

Blossoms of water chestnut delicately ornament
      autumn lotus:
lotus leaves so sparse, chestnut leaves so many!
The breeze wafts a voice through the fading sunlight:
who has composed a new "Chestnut-Picking Song"?

### 14

I leisurely paint soft jade branches
    of new bamboo groves;
at the morning window, move my brush:
    shadows grow and spread.
Just look where the moist green places
    look like banks of cloud—
you'd think it was the Hsiao and Hsiang riverlands
    after rain had passed.

MCC, 2/37a.

### 15

In the cold of the year I live my life
    among the traces of ink,
brushing forth the ice and frost,
    a feeling never exhausted.
The ancient tree is quite content
    to age among cliffs and valleys:
it has no need of "flower news" each time
    the spring winds blow.

16

Above ten thousand mountains, autumn clearing
    as morning clouds disperse;
the sound of emerald gully-streams
    echoes from tips of trees.
My brush comes here and by itself
    creates a hermitage:
surely, gathering magic fungus,
    Masters Ch'i and Huang will soon appear.

MCC, 2/37a–b. Masters Ch'i and Huang were two of the "Four Whiteheads of Shang Mountain," old men who withdrew from the turmoil of the late Ch'in dynasty.

17

Rain dissipates over misty peaks,
    ten thousand layers of blue-green;
waterfalls fly in a hundred turnings
    down mountains beneath clear sky.
The people here in residence
    live near the Valley of Master Fool:
they plant no mulberry or hemp,
    but pinetrees and bamboo.

MCC, 2/37b. Master Fool: Duke Huan of Ch'i was on a hunt when he encountered an old gentleman. He asked this man, "What valley is this?" and was answered, "It is called Master Fool's Valley." The Duke was surprised: "Why is that?" And the response came, "It is named after your humble subject." The T'ang-dynasty poet and travel essayist Liu Tsung-yüan (773–819) refers to this episode in one of his prefaces and then tells that he himself named a stream near which he lived in exile, "Fool Stream," because "I incurred guilt through my foolishness."

### 18

Hibiscus along a wattle fence,
    clusters of bamboo;
a newly thatched studio
    facing distant peaks. . . .
I laugh at myself—I just can't seem
    to get rid of my habit:
from behind a curtain of scattered rain
    I paint the autumn scene.

### 19

Arrayed in green the willow branches
    give rise to white mist;
the thatched hall gateway is tightly closed
    beside the Halfway Stream.
For two years I trod the snow
    of the capital terraces;
betraying the shadows of plum blossoms,
    while the moon was out I slept.

MCC, 2/37b–38a.

### 20

Loud we sing the White Hemp Song,
    leaning back in our boat;
a winding embankment beneath clear sky,
    trees crowded with flocks of crows.
Yellow leaves fly wildly,
    the misty waters stretch wide:
the place where the evening ripples turn red
    is where the fishermen live.

21

Moistening the green, misty clouds
    fly above, below:
these wooded mountains look just like
    a painting by Mi Yu-jen.

Astonishing! Splashed ink creates
    a storm of wind and rain;
wildly it buffets the fishing boat,
    at evening not yet home.

MCC, 2/38a–b. Mi Yu-jen (1074–1153): a famous painter of the southern Sung dynasty, known for his moist landscapes.

22

The gully falls flow down from the east,
    incomparably pure;
winding, they turn behind the bamboo,
    only their sound is heard.

Where the thatched hut stands solemn,
    a man in solitude;
frosty branches jut high up, pale mists arise.

23

In old age I've not completely given up my habit:
I love to sit at the hidden window
    beside my ink and inkstone.

Brush in hand, I never depart
    from the style of Huang Tzu-chiu:
with pale and dark strokes, playfully I paint
    a picture of Mount Yü.

MCC, 2/38b. Huang Tzu-chiu: Huang Kung-wang (1269–1354), one of the Four Masters of Yüan-dynasty painting.

### 24

Maple River's waters run chilly,
        all creatures come home early;
dreams are filled with blossoming reeds,
        autumn not abated.
A single goose does not go to sleep;
        he frolics in the moonlight:
where ripples glitter, trembling in the distance,
        the sky will soon show dawn.

### 25

The poplars white, the blossoms fly
        east of the rivers of Ch'u;
a bamboo grove takes a western turning,
        a bamboo bridge goes through.
In tiny boat, with wine on board,
        we penetrate the mist:
the entire journey in splashed ink paintings
        of Rivers Hsiao and Hsiang.

MCC, 2/38b–39a.

### 26

Beside the bridge of weeping willows,
        beyond the autumn hills,
a man heads home in a fishing boat
        to the bay of setting sun.
From the swath of flowering reeds
        a wind suddenly arises:
huddled in a raincloak, covered with blossoms like snow,
        he returns alone.

27

The forest doves summon rain
  and yet no rain appears;

the mountain magpies cry for clearing,
  but it's still not clear.

These songs of theirs, sounding all day,
  what's their real purpose?

They wish to urge the splashing of ink
  into a painting by Master Mi!

MCC, 2/39a–b. Master Mi: Mi Fu (1051–1107) and his son Mi Yu-jen, both famous for their wet landscapes based on the manipulation of moist "dots" of ink.

28

Invisible birds settle in the woods
  as evening colors fade;

I roll up the blinds on autumn shadows
  at my darkening window.

The boy I call to blow out the lamp;
  my brush-strokes are not done;

I'll wait for morning light to stipple
  the east slope of the eastern hills.

29

Why should young men think of retiring
    to a fishing pier?

Yet along Maple River I often remember
    how Chi-ying returned.

This is the time when "water-lily soup"
    and "sliced perch" are just right:

I wonder why the tip of my brush
    can't do the fish really plump.

MCC, 2/39b. Chi-ying, or Chang Han (early 4th century), was a
native of Wu (Suchou) who served under the Prince of Ch'i but grew nostal-
gic for the water-lily soup and sliced perch of his hometown, so he withdrew
from the post and returned to Wu.

30

In the mist the leaves turn yellow
    around the village estate;

a stone bridge approaches to the west
    of the Hall for Reading Books.

Most I love the fields of millet,
    the early autumn harvest:

when the wine is ready, first they boil
    purple crabs to eat.

31

Along Lien Stream the bamboo trees
      possess a lovely freshness;
here, just a hairsbreadth away,
      inspired feelings expand!
Windswept rains pass my window
      this season of ripening plums:
the inkstone is filled with black liquid
      splashing paulownia blossoms.

MCC, 2/39b–40a.

32

When spring comes to the riverside
      tree after tree renews;
white gulls, yellow orioles
      fly together now.
On all four sides of the thatch-roofed hut
      the mountains seem alive:
who will retire to this place
      and become their master?

## 33

In the river village, willows
　　show pale and show dark;

blossoms of peach, blossoms of plum
　　fly high and low, all red.

The wine is ready as I pay
　　my visit to farmers' huts:

drunk, I take my worn-out brush
　　and paint the *Odes of Pin.*

MCC, 2/40a–b. *Odes of Pin:* A reference to the first poem in the *Odes of Pin* section of the *Shih ching* ("Book of Songs"), *The Seventh Month.* This is a kind of "occupations of the months" which describes in detail various rural tasks of the seasons. The poem was often illustrated in later centuries.

## 34

At valley mouth, calmly, calmly,
　　clouds now dissipate;

pines and cedars high and low
　　naturally shape the hills.

I'm glad the thatched hut lies beyond
　　the Chung-nan mountain range:

I don't strive for ceremonial silk,
　　just let my white hair grow.

35

After rain, the morning comes,
      again it turns all dark;
from autumn cliffs the trees shed leaves,
      piling thicker, thicker.
Should an old friend from a thousand miles away
      come to visit here,
except for the sound of me reading out loud
      the place would be hard to find.

MCC, 2/40b.

36

Some willow trees adorn the gate,
      leaning at a slant;
at dawn they're brushed by hazy light,
      at evening filled by crows.
As boys I remember we'd pull off catkins,
      friends chasing after friends . . .
now, hair turned white, we're separated
      at the ends of the earth.

37

Sad and sere the bamboo grove
      leans from the river bank;
at base of rock new sedge appears,
      lapped by rippling waves.
A swath of distant mountains takes
      the sun as it sinks down;
the thatched pavilion—autumn shadows—
      quiet, no one there.

MCC, 2/40b–41a.

### 38

The village elders meet together,
    talk of rainy weather;
yesterday the swelling tides
    flooded the southern fields.
Best to sell our calves, buy boats,
    and set off on the river,
weaving nets to spread and catch
    the "shrunken-headed" bream!

### 39

At dawn they leave the thatch-roofed inn
    as snow begins to melt;
the road meanders, peaks are dense,
    each step is dangerous!
If cantilever plankways
    were as level as your hand,
Still it would be better to lie comfortable back home!

MCC, 2/41a–b.

### 40

The hoary pines snap under snow,
    wild branches hang and cross;
beside the house, the mountain hollow, beautiful,
    hemmed in.
And still he goes on teaching classics,
    past the midnight hour:
by paper window, lamp-cast shadows
    fall on chilly stairs.

MCC, 2/41b.

## Evening Travel

The sun sets over empty, empty road:
who can I turn to to ease my evening travel?
Continuing alone, mind like burning fire,
scanning all directions—the road unknown to me.
I hear birds singing—their calls are mostly strange:
they're startled and delighted to meet anyone at all.
Let me not grieve that it grows late as I go;
the mountain moon emerges from the woods ahead, all
    bright.

*San-yü chi*, p. 89.


## Dreaming of Visiting Tiger Hill

The self-chiming bell rings noon
        as I lie down to nap;
suddenly, I dream of passing
        Seven Mile Embankment.
Pleasure-seekers moor their boats,
        filled with people singing;
peddlers shoulder autumn flowers,
        busily trying to hawk them.
Evening clouds laden with rain
        rumble above Twin Wells;
mountain magpies cry for clearing,
        enlivening the terrace of stone.
The moon arrives just as I
        enjoy the chanting of poems;
I wake—in the garden courtyard
        the sun's still not gone down.

*San-yü chi*, p. 90.

## *A Rainfall*

Outside my gate, spring radiance
      is swept blank by the rain,
scattering, scattering butterflies,
      soaking fragrant flowers;
wildly driving down willow catkins
      that seem mingled with snow,
madly dropping peach-tree blossoms—
      you'd think them swept by wind!
Swelling waters pound city walls,
      pour into northern streets;
dove-calls are heard crying to their mates,
      emerging from east of the woods.
And here, I'm happy that my roof
      does not leak on my bed:
half the time I spend asleep
      in distant, distant dreams.

*San-yü chi*, p. 90.

## A Western Lantern

This lantern from distant parts is strange:

its flame has been lit from Cold Food fires.

I try viewing the scenes of Rome;
>        (—The name of the place where the Church
>                has its headquarters.)

horizontally read the Latin characters.
>        (—The West's ancient writing.)

Moths flit about the light but can't approach;

a rat peers out, his shadow all alone.

Startled, I read the missive from the West:

all these affairs, have they been heard of before?

*San-yü chi*, p. 90. Cold Food: A springtime festival. The notes to lines 3 and 4 are by the poet himself. As Fang Hao suggests, the apparatus in question must have been a type of camera obscura or related device for viewing an early version of slides. The missive mentioned in the penultimate line would presumably have been a letter accompanying the device and sent from Rome.

## Reading of Antiquity
(Three Poems from the Group of Ten)

## The Emperor of Ch'in

At Li-shan Mountain the palace is shut down,
>        the pipes and strings are silent;

he wasted effort gathering herbs,
>        his hair went on turning gray.

Had he succeeded in his search
>        for immortality,

he would have swallowed the Paradise Islands
>        before ending his campaign.

*San-yü chi*, p. 90. Li-shan: The location of the tomb of Ch'in Shih-huang-ti.

## *Ti Liang-kung*

No sooner come to govern Chiang-tung
    than he was transferred south;

he burned to the ground the decadent shrines
    turning them to smoke!

What a shame that Master Ti
    was not another Fu I

and so did not make sure the nuns
    would marry Buddhist monks!

*San-yü chi*, p. 91. Ti Jen-chieh 狄仁傑 (630–700) was a leading official of the T'ang dynasty; Liang-kung ("The Duke of Liang") was a posthumous title. Ti is the "Judge Dee" made famous by Robert Van Gulik in his translations of murder mysteries with Dee as detective, and especially in his own original mysteries also featuring Dee. Wu Li sees him as a predecessor of T'ang Pin (1627–1687), whose suppression of "decadent shrines" in 1685 was applauded by Wu and many other scholars of the day. Fu I 傅奕 was an important anti-Buddhist polemicist of the T'ang dynasty; he also wrote a commentary on the *Tao te ching*. For an excellent summation of Fu I's "Memorial Requesting the Suppression of Buddhism," submitted to the throne in 621, see Kakehi Fumio 筧文生, *Tō Sō hatsuka bun* 唐宋八家文, Vol. 20 in the series, *Kanshō Chūgoku no koten* 鑑賞中国の古典 (Tokyo: Kadokawa, 1989), pp. 91–93. Kakehi's purpose is to demonstrate the indebtedness to Fu I's arguments of the famous "Memorial on the Fingerbone of Buddha" by Han Yü (768–824).

## *Lin Ho-ching*

All alone he enjoyed withdrawal
　　from the realm of dust;
not many of his poems were left
　　to later generations.
But why did he not utterly
　　transcend relationships?
—His plum-tree wife and crane-children
　　never left the mountain!

> *San-yü chi*, p. 92. Lin Ho-ching: Lin Pu 林逋 (957–1028), one of the great early Sung-dynasty poets, famous for living the life of a recluse at West Lake with "a plum tree as his wife and cranes as his children."

## *Asking the Way in a Snowbound Village*

Hungry sparrows, cold, have much to say;
they fly and fly but never leave the village.
As snow-clouds clear, I see a bramble gate
where an old couple takes the southern sun.
I approach and ask the way ahead:
before telling me, they consult in whispers.

> *San-yü chi*, p. 92. The same poem is found at MCC, 2/31a, with a different last line: "Smiling, they point, but do not say a word."

## Sojourning Here

On spring hills the flowers bloom—
    I ride the lake beneath clear skies;
each day I bring my poet's gourd and my jug of wine.
After sojourning here for ten years,
    the excitement of wandering has dimmed;
even in painting from memory
    the picture seems obscure.

*San-yü chi*, p. 92.

# Thirty Miscellaneous Poems on Macao

### 1

At the pass, Kuang-tung ends,
    then down to level sand;
mountain formations at Hao-ching
    can be compared to flowers.
Residents! Don't be alarmed!
    I'm not here by mistake.
From afar I've come to study the Way
    at São Paulo Church!

*Poet's note:* The mountain colors are purplish-black, their forms comparable to flower buds. São Paulo is the name of the church of the Society of Jesus.
    The Chinese texts for these poems will be found in *San-pa chi*, in CKH, pp. 107–115, and in MCC, 3/45a–50a.

### 2

A bend of towers and terraces,
    five *li* along the sand:
the accents one hears everywhere
    are those of Hakka folk.
The ocean doves are really foolish,
    urging farmers on:
these people abandon the dike-fields,
    slanting beyond the waves.

*Poet's note:* The land stretches out five or six *li*; the dike fields, beyond the water, are very meager. The residents know nothing of spring plowing; they make their living from the sea.

### 3

Yellow sand, whitewashed houses: here the black men live;
willows at the gates like sedge, still not sparse in autumn.
Midnight's when the Tanka come and make their harbor
        here;
fasting kitchens for noonday meals have plenty of fresh
        fish.

*Poet's note:* The blacks by custom admire a deep black color as beautiful; a pale black they consider ugly. There are two varieties of fish: shad and *liu* fish. They are fried in Western olive oil, and then eaten for the forty-day lenten fast.

For the first four characters of the second line, the holograph reading has been followed: *men liu ju t'an*. In the poet's note, after "beautiful" (*mei*), the holograph has the phrase, *tan-che wei ch'ou*, which is translated here.

### 4

Holding candles, burning high,
        they welcome the great saint;
banners, pennants flap in wind,
        cannon roar like thunder.
On all sides streets are spread with grass,
        green like tapestry:
pedestrians are not allowed to trample it to dust.

*Poet's note:* When St. Francis Xavier [1506–1552] emerges in procession, the streets are covered with flowers and grass to show reverence. The streets are called "Awe of Majesty, Love of Virtue" (*wei-wei huai-te*).

5

Ocean vapors hover dark,
        change to evening sky:
the fishing boats moor side by side,
        cooking fires arise.
The wild geese know this place is far,
        hard to reach in flight;
the island moon tomorrow night—
        full for the year's twelfth month.

*Poet's note:* The Tanka go out in boats to catch fish, making the
ocean their home, and not returning for a full year.

6

In short plush shirts and leather shoes so light

they promenade beneath Gun Terrace Mountain
        in newly cleared weather.
Happening to meet a fellow countryman,
        they speak of the western mines:
"Recently, I fear, the yellow gold
        is less easy to extract."

*Poet's note:* By custom they like short plush shirts, with narrow
sleeves, and in the center knots on all four sides tied very tight. They
wear leather shoes, each shoe with only one clog-tooth [heel]. Those
who wear two swords—one long and one short—slanting at the
loins, and carry a red wood stick, are the military officers.

### 7

Along evening embankments they gather in the nets—
    a fishy smell from the trees!

The barbarian Tanka gather to buy wine,
    filling their jars to the brim.

At sea these days all is peaceful,
    no incidents at all:

the double doors have long been shut
    at the deserted pavilion.

*Poet's note:* Whenever some incident occurs at sea, the officials gather in this pavilion, which is called the "Pavilion for Holding Council."

### 8

Young women carefully adorn themselves,
    embroidered shawls covering them;

when would they ever expose their hairdos
    or paint their eyebrows long?

Their husbands in pursuit of profit
    often leave on trips:

with each rising of the tide
    it's time to say goodbye.

*Poet's note:* Around their homes they plant no mulberries; the women know nothing of sericulture. They cover their entire bodies in red and purple flowered embroideries with pointed peaks which they hold about themselves in such a way that the eyes and half the face are barely exposed. Those in mourning wear black.

## 9

The palm trees here provide thick shade,
    the place is never cold;
the birds sing when the springtime comes,
    the wineshops fill with cheer.
All visitors drink wine and talk
    of things in native lands;
the etiquette is much the same,
    except—they doff their hats!

*Poet's note:* Those who wear their hair in a hanging bun with gold threads favor a hat of black flannel wool; this hat is shaped like a bamboo *li*-hat. When they meet someone they doff it as a greeting.

## 10

Windswept ship, dashing quickly,
    day and night with dizzy speed:
who could lie secure in it, dreaming of his homeland?
The itinerary lies ahead—passage to the distant West!
Today they must have gone beyond the Crimson Path.

*Poet's note:* In reckoning Master Couplet's [Father Philippe Couplet (1623–1693)] itinerary, I would estimate that he must have crossed the Crimson Path [Equator].

11

At winter solstice mountain flowers
    open in profusion;
in netted chairs on carriers' shoulders
    people come to look.
Lying and viewing, one wants to ask,
    Who knows the flowers' names?
They open and fall before spring winds
    are here to urge them on.

*Poet's note:* Flowers blossom all four seasons. The traveler's palanquins are like boxes with long poles, and windows on both sides. One enters and then reclines. Those of the honored and wealthy are artfully ornamented with carved lacquer. Those of ordinary people are like a sack of netting covered with oiled cloth. Two black men carry them on their shoulders.

12

A single hair, Green Isle
    rises from the sea,
all around, blue-green colors
    and a cooling breeze.
Yesterday we went for relaxation,
    then came home quite late,
crossing waves at night that seemed
    to glitter red with fire.

*Poet's note:* Green Isle has many blue-green trees; it is a spot for enjoying the cool and relaxing. When the ocean waves swell at night, they look exactly like scattered fires or falling meteors.
    "Green Isle": According to the British traveler Peter Mundy, who visited Macao in the mid-1630s, "On the Inner side of the Citty lieth a little rocky Iland called Isla Verde or greene Iland, beelonguing to the Padres of Saint Paule, or the Jesuits, and by them was caused to bee planted, soe thatt Now in a Manner it is covered with Fruit trees and yeildeth by report 2 or 3000 Ryall off eightt yearly profitt to them." See Lt.-Col. Sir Richard Carnac Temple, ed., *The Travels of Peter Mundy in Europe and Asia, 1608–1667*, vol. 3, pt. 1 (London: Hakluyt Society, 1919), p. 269.

13

Where waves encircle the Three Mountains
　　herbs grow fragrantly;
how could they lead to the confounding
　　of several sovereign lords?
Left behind by the Ch'in gatherers
　　still they flourish, green:
the herbs themselves achieved Long Life,
　　the men are long since gone!

*Poet's note:* Three Mountains is traditionally said to be the spot
where herbs were plucked in the Ch'in and Han periods.

14

The ninth month here is without frost—
　　tangerines and citrons turn orange;
in winter's three months comes the rain,
　　ripening the loquats.
Cold-weather birds will probably not
　　come often to peck at them:
they will be saved for our pure fast
　　to accompany noontime tea.

*Poet's note:* The loquats ripen in winter; they are meager and sour.

### 15

Before Cross Gate the sun
    moves on towards the twilight;
at Chiu-chou, colored mists scatter,
    at evening all is haze.
A man who passes these two spots
    should not look back at them:
where vision ends, among the dust,
    tears easily exhausted.

*Poet's note:* Cross Gate faces Chiu-chou. When Li I-shan [Li Shang-yin 李商隱 (813?–858)] wrote in a poem, "I've only heard beyond the sea there is a place, Chiu-chou," he was referring to this spot. If you gaze at it from afar, it seems to disappear and then reappear, like nine blue spirals in the distance.

### 16

A rainbow shows tomorrow morning
    wild typhoons will blow;
and fish that swallow boats down whole
    are swimming back and forth!
I wonder—after 90,000 *li*
    of windswept waves,
when he's back home, with whom will he
    converse of life and death?

*Poet's note:* This refers to Mr. Lo going to the Greater West. [Fang Hao speculates that "Mr. Lo" may be the Portuguese Jesuit, Balthasar-Didacus de Rocha.]

17

From the second story of this building
        I hear them on three sides:
the ocean waves, on windless days,
        still sounding out like thunder!
In coming and going, finally
        I yield to the sea gulls:
let me preserve their flying flocks
        by painting them onto a screen.

*Poet's note:* This storied building has three floors; I sleep and eat on the second.

18

Boats come from the Lesser West;
        merchants already know:
they come to purchase foreign peppers,
        their shouts disturbing the twilight!
For ten days in confusion
        they crowd the road of sand,
bearers, both "black" and "white,"
        flock after flock of them.

*Poet's note:* When goods from the Lesser West arrive in Macao, bearers wrangle in confusion for positions on the road.

### 19

At the tips of red lichee branches
      the moon again goes west;
I rise and watch the wind-swept dew,
      my eyes still all confused.
Before the lamp, this place is not
      a scholar's studio:
I only hear the sound of bells,
      I hear no rooster's crow.

*Poet's note:* Dusk and dawn are marked only by the sound of the "self-sounding bell."

### 20

Winter nights seem one year long,
      though shorter in the cold;
old bedclothes must be thrown on top,
      the clothes we wear are warm.
From the front mountain and the ridge behind
      a single sound of bells,
snapping awake the man of the Way
      from his idle dreams.

*Poet's note:* When the little bell of the Holy Mother Chapel on the front mountain begins to strike, the large bells of the various churches ring in response.

21

In deepest winter, there does not fall
      one flake of auspicious snow;
it's always like the Season of Plums,
      rain moistening robe and shirt.
Up in my tower every day I sit
      and smell the dragon vapors
as the pond's surface rises and rises
      with salty ocean rain.

*Poet's note:* During the cold season the trees do not wither, and there
is no frost or snow at all.

22

Where the wild mountains are highest,
      alone I explore secret places;
from below my clogs, a muddy smell;
      I'm frightened of tigers hidden deep.
Why do clouds obscure the road
      that leads back through the pass?
—They fear that if I see it,
      homesick feelings will arise.

*Poet's note:* If you climb the high mountain at the pass, you can see
Kuangtung in the distance.

### 23

When you've passed beyond Yü Ridge,
        there are no more flowering plums;
for half a year, my mysterious feelings
        have been entrusted to my brush.
Yesterday's painting, now I send
        to friends along the River Lung:
at windows in clear weather,
        they will unroll it and gaze.

*Poet's note:* For a long time I have seen no plums; alone I have climbed blossomless ridges.

### 24

I always sigh in autumn wind—
        we parted from Fisherman's Jetty:
my two children like swallows, each
        went flying off.
And so I must expect that we remember at this season;
at River Che about this time the perch
        are fattening up.

*Poet's note:* At this time, my children are in Hang-chou.

25

"Natural Philosophy"—hard to meet up with
    teachers from abroad;
those from afar who pursue it here—
    all of them are children.
Why is it they divide daily classes
    between *mao* and *yu*?
—They hear the bell's gentle ringing
    and study only at these two times.

*Poet's note:* The schools are divided into Higher School and Lower School. The only class times are at the two periods of *mao* [5–7 A.M.] and *yu* [5–7 P.M.]. They ring a bronze bell to signal the start of class.

    "*Hsing hsüeh*" 性學 in the first line is the Chinese term used by the Jesuits to translate "Natural Philosophy" (as opposed to Theology). The first line may mean that there are few teachers of Natural Philosophy available; those who do live in Macao are busy teaching the children (line 2).

26

In lamplight, our native tongues, one West and one East:
when we don't understand, we can still use the brush
    and thus converse.
I write my fly-head words and you, your words like legs of
    flies;
read horizontally or vertically, so hard to penetrate!

*Poet's note:* The Western characters are like fly-legs; they are written horizontally. In reading them out loud, a sharp, high pitch is considered best.

### 27

A thousand lanterns glitter from a cliff of tiny trees:
brocades forming cloudy peaks, candles forming flowers.
They decorate these winter mountains and all come to
        enjoy:
black men's dancing feet keep time to the guitar!

*Poet's note:* The winter mountains are made of wood formed into the
underlying rock, brocaded cloth as mountain peaks, dyed candles of
red and blue as flowers and trees. In form it is like a tortoise mountain. When the blacks sing, they move their feet in a dance which
keeps time with the sounds of the guitar. This all takes place around
the time of Jesus's birth.

### 28

As one grows old, who can bring back
        the time when he was young?
I work so hard, day after day,
        but fear I'm much too slow.
I think of my old practice,
        wish to burn up my inkstone
and then stop smearing crow-marks
        and give up poetry.

*Poet's note:* I have received firm permission to study the Way.

## 29

My journey west did not take place—
    how do I feel now?

Stuck in Macao through two seasons each
    of winter and of spring!

Tomorrow again I'll inquire about the crossing
    over Fragrant Mountain,

past the ridge beside the plum trees
    where water routes are many.

*Poet's note:* Master Po [Couplet] invited me to accompany him to the Great West, but after we reached Macao, it did not work out.

Fang Hao dates this poem to 1682. The last two lines may represent the poet's thoughts of returning north through Kuangtung province.

## 30

The river route—now cloudy, now clear,
    so hard to keep track of the weather!

My returning sail moves quite slowly
    as we approach Nan-ch'ang.

The boatmen recognize the traveler
    who came down in winter;

they tell me the springtime current
    is stronger than before.

*Poet's note:* Along my return route, it rained profusely. The river rose and so we traveled cautiously.

Nan-ch'ang: In northern Chianghsi province, approached from the south by the River Kan. The third line apparently refers to a previous trip taken by Wu Li from Macao; the present poem presumably describes his final departure.

# Poems on Christian Themes in Classical Shih Form

## *Lamentable*

Human life, disorderly!
Men grieve at poverty, low station,
      not that they lack the Way!
So hurried, the parting of death;
it waits not for teeth loosening,
      head turning completely bald.
Life and death a muddle, and no one
      understands:
Unless you learn to become aware,
      for certain you will boil and seethe!
Branching out chaotically,
      detours lead astray;
men stay confused so long, not just
      because of hair turned frost.
Confucian scholars too quite often
      fall into this trap,
and yet they mock the Heavenly Learning
      for deficiency in right reason.
They only seem like wandering sheep
      who've lost the road back home;
one never sees them find the Way
      by following repentance.
Time is running out—it flies faster than an arrow;
no matter whether short or long,
      there's no escaping death.
If you do not accord a hairsbreadth
      with what is transcendent by nature
when your coffin is covered over
      your sin will go on forever!
Today, for whom am I ringing my bell
      from one village to the next?

Ten years I've been stumbling along,
    tirelessly in motion.
How can I get a thousand hamlets, ten thousand villages,
all to turn themselves towards the Way,
    to gain new life from death?

*San-yü chi*, p. 92.

## Song of the Fisherman

From patching rips in tattered nets
    his eyes have gotten blurred;
he scours the river, does not disdain
    the tiniest fish and shrimp.
Selecting the freshest, he has supplied
    the feasts of sovereigns;
all four limbs exhausted now,
    dare he refuse the work?
Spreading nets he gets confused
    by water just like sky;
song lingering, still drunk, approaches
    dragons as they sleep.
Now hair and whiskers are all white,
    his face has aged with time;
he's startled by the wind and waves
    and fears an early autumn.
Some friends of his have changed their job:
    they now are fishers of men;
he hears, compared to fishing fish,
    this task is tougher still.
Of late he finds the Heavenly Learning
    has come into the city:
to customers now happily add families that fast.

*San-yü chi*, p. 102.

## *Sent to Kuo*

The gate of eternal blessings
      this day has opened for you;
the light of grace and felicitation
      have come to you from Heaven.

Extirpated are your former taints,
      repulsed the Devil's troops;
now you will enjoy the real bread,
      formed in the Holy Womb.

How dignified! Your name has entered
      the register of the righteous.

How glorious! Your heart
      becomes an altar for the Lord.

I know you will prove worthy
      to console the people's yearning;
the great hall now is in need of pillars
      raised on rock.

---

MCC, 3/53a–b. *Note by Li Ti*: We do not know Kuo's personal name. Nor do we know where he came from. At the time, he had received baptism and taken the Holy Bread [the Eucharist]. The Master [Wu Li] wrote this poem to congratulate him.

## *Singing of the Source and Course of Holy Church*

### 1

Within the twelvefold walled enclosure,
    at the highest spot
is the palace of the Lord
    with springs and autumns of its own.
The misty fragrance is breath of flowers
    where roses bloom;
the glittering brilliance is glow of pearls
    where gemmed crowns reverently bow.
There in Heaven should we seek
    true blessings and true joy;
in the human realm we must cut off
    false strivings and false plans.
Look there where girls, so many of them,
    their hair in tufts,
day after day follow behind
    the Holy Mother in their play.

MCC, 3/59a.

2

Before the firmament was ever formed,
  or any foundation laid,

high there hovered the Judge of the World,
  prepared for the last days!

This single Man from His five wounds
  poured every drop of blood;

a myriad nations gave their hearts
  to the wonder of the Cross!

The heavenly gates now have a ladder
  leading to their peace;

demonic spirits lack any art
  to insinuate deception.

Take up the burden, joyfully
  fall in behind Jesus,

look up with reverence towards the top of that mountain,
  follow His every step.

MCC, 3/59b.

3

Primal chaos of myriad ages—
    orifices were bored, breath blown into them.

The single globule of earth
    rolled among heavenly powers and bodies.

Flowers flourished, cicadas droned,
    in perfect correspondence;

snow darkened sky, wind fiercely blew,
    each quite unawares.

In the Old Testament
    there was no essence of life;

the spiritual source had in store
    another wondrous proposal.

These words of advice and admonishment
    retain, Sir, in your ear:

imprint them against the time when you
    will have no words to say.

4

One day, when a baby boy came down to earth,
He had not the slightest sin;
     now such a thing is rare!
From Heaven He descended,
     how blessed, oh how blessed!
By a woman he was born,
     how wondrous, oh how wondrous!
All the saints sighed in admiration,
     stretched forward for a look;
the myriad regions leapt and danced,
     joy in all expressions.
The one once promised to be with us has come to comfort
     us: remember

*Translator's note:* I am unable to determine the meaning of the last line.

5

I used to chant that poem of Chou
    about "ascending and descending":
it was like clouds or fog dispersing,
    so I could see the azure sky.
I never suspected a world of brilliance
    double that of sun and moon
would start with the year *keng-shen*
    of the *Yüan-shou* reign.
Learning then had new knowledge
    with blessings pure imbued;
the Way attained far-reaching care,
    the holy work complete.
I wish to follow cloud-pendants of jade
    to hear exalted singing;
how could the pearl of the black dragon alone
    serve to illuminate that poem?

*Translator's note:* The translation of the last line is tentative; I am uncertain of the relevant allusion.

6

By nature I have always felt quite close to the Way;
when done with chanting my new poems,
     I always concentrate my spirit.

Prior to death, who believes
     in the joy of the land of Heaven?

After the end, then comes amazement
     at the truth of the fires of hell!

The achievements and fame of this ephemeral world:
     footprints of geese on snow;

this body, this shell in a lifetime of toil:
     dust beneath horses' hoofs.

And what is more, the flowing of time
     presses man so fast:

let us plan to ask carefully about the ford
     that leads to the true source.

7

Teeth and hair infused with spirit—
      this we call a man;

the great Father of all heaven and earth
      is the truth in human nature.

At last we know the "fern" supreme;
      the heavenly task is clear.

This indeed is the "orchid terrace"
      the child is meant to seek out.

For past events we deeply grieve,
      a thousand gallons of tears!

Future happiness is surely foretold,
      spring in every season!

Not merely because of favoring a teaching
      have we started a new teaching:

let us strive for faith that we shall live forever
      in blessings and in peace.

*Translator's note:* The translation of lines 3 and 4 is tentative and based on the assumption that Wu Li intends allusions to poem 14 in the *Shih ching* and to the lost *Shih ching* poem, *Nan-kai* 南陔. The former poem associates the plucking of ferns with longing for a lord whom the speaker is missing (or has not yet met). Karlgren translates the key lines as follows: "I ascend that southern mountain, I gather the *wei* plant; when I have not yet seen the lord, my heart is pained, but when I have seen him, when I have met him, my heart is at ease." See Bernhard Karlgren, *The Book of Odes* (Stockholm: Museum of Far Eastern Antiquities, 1950), p. 9. The preface to the lost *Nan-kai* poem links it with *hsiao* (filial piety) and *yu* (friendship). The third-century scholar Shu Hsi 束晳 wrote a poem to take the place of this lost ode, which includes the lines *hsün pi nan kai, / yen ts'ai ch'i lan* 循彼南陔言采其蘭 ("I seek that southern terrace, / indeed to pluck the orchid there"). See Morohashi Tetsuji, *Daikanwa jiten* (Tokyo: 1955–1959), 2:1648–1649. It seems possible that Wu Li's use of these allusions is intended to suggest that Christ is the true Lord and his father the true Father and friend, but this interpretation must remain tentative.

### 8

In the very highest place, deep within a mansion
dwells a family perfectly united, loving and devoted.
Beyond past, beyond present, the three Persons are one;
penetrating heaven, penetrating earth,
       the one family is three!
Those who are known as "daily improving"
       to praise the Spirit are worthy;
the world possesses a wondrous flower
       fit to protect the holy.
On painted walls, year after year,
       we contemplate their images:
pure incense rises in orderly spirals
       to where their noses inhale.

### 9

In glory they are crowned in jade,
       and clothed in robes of gold;
their merit earned in bloody battle,
       childlike their hearts.
A valley of ten thousand colors,
       fragrances and flowers;
a forest from a single root,
       a single trunk and vine.
To soul's repletion, intoxicated
       they drink from the cup of Jesus;
with dancing limbs, they stretch forward to listen
       to the harp of David.
"Holy, Holy, Holy," their voices ceaselessly cry:
beneath the throne of the Lamb
       echoes the sound of their song.

10

Utterly transcendent, His wondrous essence
        was never limited to place;
to bring life to the teeming people
        He showed Himself, then hid.
Effortlessly, a single standard—
        a new cake baked for us;
as before, the six directions have one supreme Lord.
In the human realm, now we have
        a whole burnt offering;
in Heaven for eternity is preserved our daily bread.
I have incurred so many transgressions,
        yet am allowed to draw near:
with body and soul fully sated,
        tears moisten my robe.

11

"The Supreme Ultimate contains three"—
        muddled words indeed!
In fact, they start with primal energy
        to speak of original chaos.
From books of the past, we learned of old
        of sincerity, wisdom, and goodness;
the mysterious meaning now we understand
        of Father, Son, and Holy Spirit.
The Persons distinct: close at hand, consider
        the flame within the mirror;
the Essence is whole: far off, please note
        the wheel that graces the sky.
The Holy Name has been revealed,
        His authority conferred;
throughout the world in this human realm,
        the sound of the teaching supreme!

12

The flower of the twelvefold heavens
    ornaments the colored clouds,
crown jewel for a new knit robe
    worthy of the Holy Mother.
The hues have been bestowed
    from the midst of light with no beginning;
the fragrance has been absorbed
    from the love of the primordial womb.
Miraculous, that a single Virgin
    should give blossom to this precious bloom;
glorious, that ten thousand saints
    should throng towards the splendid audience!
What day will we receive the blessing
    of entering His court,
His beauteous visage ourselves to see,
    each face suffused with joy?

*Translator's note:* The translation of line 6 is tentative.

## From "Moved to Sing of the Truth of Holy Church"

### 5

The Grand Music in Harmonious Heaven plays;
in joyful leaping, there gather all the saints!
Instruments blowing, the gold trumpet sounds;
tones harmonizing, phoenix and lion conduct.
This "inner scene" has limitless light;
the True Flower is endlessly fragrant.
In this place a single day
is a thousand years in the ordinary world.

MCC, 3/57b–58a.


## Overcoming Pride

The evil of pride—would you know what it is like?
An arrogant lion, untamable!
With strong heart he boasts of what he possesses;
looks down around as if there were no one else.
For a few days he pierces the clouds on high,
then falls to the dust for a thousand autumns.
How diligently to overcome this in oneself?
Of ten thousand virtues, one––humility—rings true.

MCC, 3/61b.

# Poems on Christian Themes in Ch'ü ("Aria") Form

## From *"Music for the Mass"*
*—to the tune,* Tung-ou ling

Again he washes his hands,
and then turns around.
He prays that he and all assembled sinners
may be washed clean with no iota left:
only then may they not betray
Jesus's compassion.
Why does he make the sign of the Cross
       over and over again?
The holy death took place nailed thereon.

(CKH, p. 70)

*From "Music of Harmonious Heaven in Reverent*
*Thanks to the Lord of Heaven"*
*—to the tune,* Hsi ch'ien ying

Late in Han

God's Son came down from Heaven

to save us people

and turn us towards the good.

His grace goes wide!

Taking flesh through the virginity
          of the Holy Mother,
               in a stable He was born.

Joseph too came to present Him in the temple:

there to offer praise was

Simeon.

They say He can

save our souls from their destructiveness

and sweep away the devil's wantonness.

(p. 73)

*From "Musical Stanzas to Admonish the Proud"*
—*to the tune,* Sheep on the Mountain Slope

Men in a dream,
unhumble, unforgiving;
bodies in illness,
undoctored and uncured.
The heaven in our nature
we let wither away;
our souls in fallen state,
faded—where are they now?
But the Lord came down from Heaven
to show His grace in the distant West,
removing the sins of the world,
the sins of the world from the beginning
washed away.
And feeling compassion on us all,
to save and take our souls!
But Oh
we living creatures still cling to delusion,
truly insane!
We are the devil's slaves
all unawares.

(p. 76)

## From "On Rules and Statutes"
—*to the tunes,* Music for the Spring *and* Victorious Music

I have heard the heavenly country
was our native land.
First evil born with
Eve and Adam:
how could they lack this ill?
Crossing Heaven, gleaning sin—who could pull them
  back?
And so all souls
did evil, deserved punishment.
It moved the One Lord,
but His mercy then was hard to count upon!

Therefore Jesus
came down and was born,
came down to save us and redeem
ten thousand countries, distant places.

(p. 79)

### *Moses Admonishes the People—Musical Stanzas*

When Moses was done with his final testament, he continued
in song and admonished the people, saying:

This wilderness!
If only you, His people,
      acknowledge one Lord of Heaven—
there is no second one!—
the Lord of Heaven will confer that rich and fertile land
to care for and to cultivate.

That land is luxuriant, fruitful,
      impossible to match!
The five grains profusely grow,
      there are no weeds and tares;
and it is even richer
in tender kid, fine wine.

Milk and honey, meat and oil, there do overflow!
The Lord of Heaven loves you as His children:
who could foresee that you, once full and sated,
      would act like animals,
kicking, biting back!
—forgetting His great gift.

(p. 81)

# Sample Chinese Texts

## *Poems 3 and 4 from "Miscellaneous Poems on Macao"*

嶴中雜咏

3 黃沙白屋黑人居

　門柳如荼秋不疏

　夜半蜑船來泊此

　齋厨午飯有鮮魚

（原註：黑人俗尚深黑為美，淡者為醜。魚有鱠鰡兩種，用太西阿里襪油炙之，供四旬齋素。）

The underlined passages follow Wu Li's holograph—see Plate 4.

4 捧蠟高燒迎聖來

　旗幢風滿砲成雷

　四街鋪草青如錦

　未許遊人踏作埃

（原註：沙勿略聖人出會，滿街鋪花與草為敬，街名畏威懷德。）

## Song of the Fisherman

漁父吟

破網修多兩眼花；淘河不厭細魚蝦。
採鮮曾進君王膳；四體雖勞敢辭倦。
撒網常迷水似天；歌殘醉傍蛟龍眠。
髯髭白盡丰姿老；驚遍風潮怕秋早。
朋儕改業去漁人；聞比漁魚更苦辛。
晚知天學到城府；買魚喜有守齋戶。

## From "Music of Harmonions Heaven in Reverent Thanks to the Lord of Heaven"
### —to the tune, Hsi ch'ien ying

喜遷鶯

自漢季，聖子來降，敦吾人，
向化明艮。恩廣。託聖母童貞產馬房。
若瑟同來獻主堂。祝讚有，
西默盎。道能救靈魂淪喪，
掃魔鬼猖狂。

## *Moses Admonishes the People*

每瑟諭眾樂章

（原注：）每瑟遺命已畢，乃賡歌而諭眾曰

荒野地。厥民惟認一天主，

無有二，天主乃特賜彼膏腴地，

照護引治。厥地裕豐難比偶。

五穀滋生無稂莠。更饒益，

羊羔美酒。乳蜜膏油多且有。

天主愛爾如厥子。誰料飽飫如

生口，施蹄齧，忘高厚。

## *Singing of the Source and Course of Holy Church (Complete Sequence)*

誦聖會源流

1 十二重寰最上頭；主宮別自有春秋。

氤氳花氣開玫瑰；燦爛珠光拜晃旒。

天上欲求真福樂；人間須斷假營謀。

試觀多少髫齡女；日日追隨聖母遊。

2 未畫開天問始基；高懸判世指終期。

一人血注五傷盡；萬國傾心十字奇。

閶闔有梯通淡蕩；妖魔無術逞迷離。

仔肩好附耶穌後；仰止山巔步步隨。

3 萬古鴻濛鑿竅吹；一丸土塊走儀羲。

花榮蟬噪全相應；雪暗風饕各不知。

故簡中無生活趣；靈源別有主張奇。

長言爛語留君耳；印取無言不語期。

4 一日嬰兒墮地時;庶無罪悔盖難之。
　自天而降福哉福;由女以生奇矣奇。
　羣聖吁嗟勞引領;萬方舞蹈喜開眉。
　與偕昔許今來慰;記取陽回四綫期。

5 曾咏周詩陟降篇;如開雲霧覩青天。
　不圖日月重光世;却在庚申元壽年。
　學有知新純睱借;道歸遠處聖功圓。
　願隨霞珮聽高唱;豈獨驪珠耀一篇。

6 性理由來與道親;新詩吟罷一凝神。
　死前誰信天鄉樂;了後方驚獄火真。
　浮世功名鴻爪雪;勞生軀殼馬蹄塵。
　流光況復催人急;擬向真原細問津。

7 齒髮含靈號曰人;乾坤大父性中真。
　始知薇極天功亮;壹是蘭陔子職循。
　往事深悲千斛淚;來歡占斷四時春。
　不緣寵教開新教;爭信常生禔福身。

8 最高之處府潭潭;眷屬團圓樂且耽。
　無古無今三位一;徹天徹地一家三。
　人名日益稱神可;世有奇花保聖堪。
　晝壁年年瞻配像;淨香理略鼻頭參。

9 榮加玉冕錫衣金;血戰功勞赤子心。
　萬色萬香萬花谷;一根一幹一萄林。
　牣靈飫飲耶穌爵;躍體傾聽達味琴。
　聖聖聖聲呼不斷;羔羊座下唱酬音。

10　超超妙體本無方；為活蒸民顯復藏。
　　宛爾一規新餅餌；依然六合大君王。
　　人間今有全燔胙；天上恒存日用糧。
　　曾是多慙容接近；形神飫處淚沾裳。

11　太極含三是漫然；真從元氣說渾淪。
　　殘篇昔識誠明善；奧義今知父子神。
　　位別近參含火鏡；體全遙指麗天輪。
　　聖名顯示權相付；普地人間至教音。

12　十二天葩綴彩曇；晃旒新製母儀堪。
　　色從無始光中賦；香自初胎寵裡含。
　　奇絕一貞開寶蕊；榮超萬聖簇華參。
　　何當受福朝元日；瑰麗親瞻面面涵。

# Notes

1. Eugene Feifel, trans., Ch'en Yüan, "Wu Yü-shan—in Commemoration of the 250th Anniversary of His Ordination to the Priesthood in the Society of Jesus," *Monumenta Serica* 3 (1938):130–170; original in *Fu-jen hsüeh-chih* 輔仁學誌, 5(1–2) (1936); and *Nien-p'u* of Wu Li, *Fu-jen hsüeh-chih* 6(1–2) (1937), reprinted in CKH. (The reprint in CKH is cited here.) See also Ch'en's brief essay, "*Wu Yü-shan ju ching chih ch'ou-tso*" 吳漁山入京之酬酢, in *Ch'en Yüan hsüeh-shu lun-wen chi, ti erh chi* 學術論文集, 第二集 (Peking: Chunghua shu-chü, 1982), pp. 272–275.

2. See the relevant articles by Fang Hao (reprinted in CKH) and Wang Tsung-yen (written especially for CKH), in CKH, pp. 69–116, 124–130, 141–146; and John W. Witek, S.J., review of CKH and another book by Chou K'ang-hsieh, *Archivum Historicum Societatis Iesu*, 44 (1975):186–188. Laurence C. S. Tam, *Six Masters of Early Qing and Wu Li* (Hong Kong Museum of Art, 1986), passim, makes use of some of the poems as biographical sources, as does Chang Feng-chen 張奉箴 in his article, "Ch'ingch'u liu ta hua-chia chih i Ye-su hui-shih Wu Yü-shan," 清初六大畫家之一耶穌會士吳漁山 *Kao-hsiung shih-ta hsüeh-pao* 高雄師大學報 1991, no. 2, pp. 117–157.

3. Teng Chih-ch'eng, *Ch'ing-shih chi-shih ch'u-pien* (Shanghai: Ku-chi ch'upan-she, 1984; reprint of Chung-hua shu-chü publication of 1965), 1:85–86.

4. The Chang Yün-chang biography is reprinted in MCC, 1/3a–4b.

5. As quoted by Chu I-tsun 朱彝尊 (1629–1709), *Ming-shih tsung* 明詩綜 (Taipei: Shih-chieh shu-chü reprint of 1962), 1:26/1a.

6. MCC, 2/15b–16a. For more on Yü Huai, see the entry by Fang Chaoying in Arthur W. Hummel, ed., *Eminent Chinese of the Ch'ing Period* (Taipei: Ch'eng-wen Publishing Co., 1975; reprint of 1943 publication), p. 942; and Richard E. Strassberg, *The World of K'ung Shang-jen: A Man of Letters in Early Ch'ing China* (New York: Columbia University Press, 1983), p. 394.

7. Albert Chan, S.J., entry on Wu Li in *New Catholic Encyclopedia* (New York: McGraw-Hill, 1967), 14:1046.

8. Wang Shih-min, *Wang Feng-ch'ang shu hua t'i-pa* 王奉常書畫題跋 (edition with preface dated 1910, T'ung-chou ou-po-lo shih 通州甌鉢羅室), *hsia* 下 / 19b–20a.

9. The context suggests that Hsü Ch'ing-yü played a role in the creation of this work, and indeed, as revealed by descriptions of the scroll in painting catalogs, Hsü wrote a poem of his own "harmonizing with the rhymes" of Wu Li's poem. Wang Shih-yüan 汪士元, in the catalog of his collection entitled *Lu-yün-lou shu hua chi-lüeh* 麓雲樓書畫記略 (undated and unpaginated; xeroxed copy in the Library of the Freer and Sackler Galleries, Washington, D.C.), states that the scroll bears inscriptions by Hsü Chih-chien, a certain Hou Chü-yüan 侯秬園, and Wang Shih-min (presumably the colophon under discussion) [p. 34a]. Hou Chü-yüan is identified by Chang Feng-chen as a certain Hou Fang 汸 on the basis of Ch'en Yüan, *Nien-p'u*, p. 10 top (see Chang Feng-chen, pp. 124 and 126). Hou Fang is probably a relative of the Hou K'ai-kuo 開國, *tzu* Ta-nien 大年, anthologized in Shen Te-ch'ien 沈德潛 et al., *Ch'ing-shih pieh-ts'ai chi* 清詩別裁集 (Shanghai: Ku-chi ch'u-pan-she, 1984), 1:310; Wu Li has a poem addressed to this man (MCC, 2/32a). Ch'ung I 崇彝, in his *Hsüan-hsüeh-chai shu hua yü-mu chi* 選學齋書畫寓目記 (1921; microfilm in the Freer-Sackler Library, *shang* 上 /20a–21a), relates how he saw the painting in Wang Shih-yüan's collection; he then records that "after [the main portion of the scroll] on a separate piece of paper there is a poem by Hsü Ch'ing-yü harmonizing with the rhymes [of Wu Li's poem]."

10. These phrases come from poem 259, *Sung kao* 崧高, in the *Ta ya* 大雅 section of the *Shih ching* 詩經. The translations given here combine Arthur Waley, *The Book of Songs* (New York: Grove Press, n.d., reprint of 1937 publication), p. 135; and Bernhard Karlgren, *The Book of Odes* (Stockholm: Museum of Far Eastern Antiquities, 1950), p. 228.

11. See reference in Fang Chao-ying, entry on Wu Li in Hummel, *Eminent Chinese*, pp. 875–877; and two essays by Ch'en Yüan, "Hsü Chih-chien i-shih" 許之漸軼事, in *Ch'en Yüan hsüeh-shu lun-wen chi, ti i chi* 第一集 (Peking: Chung-hua shu-chü, 1980), pp. 187–188; and "Wu Yü-shan yü Hsü Ch'ing-yü" 吳漁山與許青嶼, in *Ch'en Yüan shih-hsüeh lun-chu hsüan* 史學論著選 (Shanghai: Jen-min ch'u-pan-she, 1981), pp. 403–405. In the second of these essays, Ch'en notes the Wang Shih-min colophon and dates the painting in question to 1674. He also rejects the attribution to Hsü of the preface to the book of Catholic teachings, *T'ien-hsüeh ch'uan-kai* 天學傳槩, the work which infuriated Yang Kuang-hsien. Jacques Gernet, *China and the Christian Impact—a Conflict of Cultures* (Cambridge: Cambridge University Press, 1982), p. 130, apparently takes Hsü's authorship for granted and proceeds to quote Yang's polemic against him at length. For the *T'ien-hsüeh ch'uan-kai*, I consulted a photostat in the Library of Congress of a copy in the Vatican Biblioteca Apostolica. For Yang's diatribe, I consulted the copy of the 1929 printing of his *Pu-te-i* 不得已 in the Library of Congress. This book contains the text in question, a letter addressed to "Consor Hsü Ch'ing-yü." For an excellent discussion of the *T'ien-hsüeh ch'uan-kai* and Yang's attack on it, but without reference to Hsü

Chih-chien, see D. E. Mungello, *Curious Land: Jesuit Accommodation and the Origins of Sinology* (Honolulu: University of Hawaii Press, 1989), pp. 92ff.

12. Ch'en Yüan, "Wu Yü-shan yü Hsü Ch'ing-yü," pp. 405–406. For the painting and translations of the colophons, see Roderick Whitfield, *In Pursuit of Antiquity* (Princeton: Princeton University Art Museum, 1974), pp. 212ff. The conversion of Hsü to Christianity is mentioned in a catalog entry by Ku Wen-pin 顧文彬 (1811–1889) in the 1882 catalog of Ku's collection, *Kuo-yün-lou shu hua chi* 過雲樓書畫記 (copy in the Freer-Sackler Library, *hua* 畫, 6a–7a). Ku writes, "Together they [Wu Li and Hsü Chih-chien] entered the Western teaching." But the colophon by Ku which is attached to the present scroll is entirely different from the printed one and does not refer to Hsü's alleged conversion. It is possible that Ku Wen-pin's catalog entry was never intended to be a colophon for actual inscription on the painting, and that Ch'en Yüan is therefore wrong in referring to it as a "colophon."

13. P'an Ching-cheng 潘景鄭, ed., *Chiang-yün-lou t'i-pa* 絳雲樓題跋 (Collected colophons of Ch'ien Ch'ien-i; Shanghai: Chung-hua shu-chü, 1958), p. 140.

14. Ch'ien Ch'ien-i, *Yu-hsüeh chi* 有學集 (edition dated 1910, Sui-Han-chai 邃漢齋), 42/7b–8a.

15. MCC, 2/13a–b. T'ang Yü-chao also inscribed a *chüeh-chü* poem on a hanging scroll by Wu Li published by Ōmura Seigai 大村西崖 in *Bunjin gasen* 文人畫選 (Tokyo: Tansei-sha, 1921–1922), vol. 2, fasc. 2, no. 14 (unpaginated). The text of T'ang's inscription indicates that Wu Li had specifically requested him to write this poem.

16. See T'an Cheng-pi 譚正璧, *Chung-kuo wen-hsüeh-chia ta tz'u-tien* 中國文學家大辭典 (Taipei: Shih-chieh shu-chü reprint, 1971), vol. 2, entry 5304 on p. 1342. T'ang's forty poems "In Imitation of Palace Lyrics" were examined in the edition of the *Chieh-yüeh shan-fang hui-ch'ao* 借月山房彙鈔 (dated 1812) in the Library of the Jimbun Kagaku Kenkyū-jo, Kyoto University.

17. Ch'en Yüan makes the point that 1668 is the year of earliest documented contact between Wu Li and Hsü Chih-chien. See his essay, "Wu Yü-shan yü Hsü Ch'ing-yü," p. 404.

18. See T'an Cheng-pi, entry 5548 on pp. 1407–1408; Teng Chih-ch'eng, *Ch'ing-shih chi-shih*, 1:441–442; Shen Te-ch'ien et al., *Ch'ing-shih pieh-ts'ai-chi*, 1:372–374. The preface is at MCC, 2/14a–b.

19. This is a reference to the famous evaluation of T'ao Ch'ien in the *Shih-p'in* 詩品 of Chung Jung. See Helmut Martin, comp., *Index to the Ho Collection of Twenty-Eight Shih-hua with a Punctuated Edition of the Ho Collection of Twenty-Eight Shih-hua* (Taipei: Chinese Materials and Research Aids Service Center, 1973), 1:13.

20. Ch'en Yü-chi, *Hsüeh-wen-t'ang wen-chi* 學文堂文集, in the *Ch'ang-chou hsien-che i-shu* 常州先哲遺書 (preface dated 1686), 3/12a–13a (Wu Wei-yeh);

3/13a–b (Wang Shih-chen); 3/13b–14b (Shih Jun-chang). The Wu Li preface is at 2/23b–24a, but with significant differences of wording.

21. The Kyoto National Museum possesses a hanging scroll by Wu Li entitled "The Growth of Auspicious Fungus at the Ts'en-wei Residence" (*Ts'en-wei-chü ch'an chih t'u* 岑蔚居產芝圖), which bears two inscriptions by Wu Li himself, dated 1659 and 1661, one by Ch'ien Ch'ien-i dated 1660, and an undated one by Wu Wei-yeh. The painting is reproduced here as Plate 1. According to Osvald Sirén, *Chinese Painting: Leading Masters and Principles* (London: Lund, Humphries, 1956, 1958), 7:446, this painting is published in the catalog of the collection of Ueno Seiichi 上野精一, *Yūchikusai* 有竹齋 (12), which I have not seen. A tiny reproduction appears in Suzuki Kei 鈴木敬, *Comprehensive Illustrated Catalogue of Chinese Paintings* (Tokyo: University of Tokyo Press, 1982), 3:190 (JM 11-007). I have been able to study the painting itself. The Wu Wei-yeh inscription consists of a prose text addressed to the man at whose home the fungus appeared, Chang Ch'un-p'ei 張春培. Although the mere presence of this text on the picture does not prove a personal relationship between Wu Li and Wu Wei-yeh, it may imply one. More suggestive is the poem inscribed by Wu Wei-yeh on Wu Li's *Picture of Reposing in the Snow* (*Wo-hsüeh t'u* 臥雪圖), the same painting inscribed by T'ang Yü-chao and published by Ōmura Seigai (see note 15). (This poem does not appear to be recorded in Wu Wei-yeh's collected works.) In a note brushed in small characters at the end of the poem, Wu Wei-yeh writes: "Yü-shan painted this picture for Mo Kung 默公." "Mo Kung" is the Buddhist monk Mo-jung 默容 (d. 1672), with whom Wu Li was friends. The fact that Wu Wei-yeh here refers to Wu Li by name may indicate that the two men actually knew each other.

Finally, Wu Li has a series of three poems following the rhymes of three poems by Wu Wei-yeh from a set of five, "On the Road to Kao-yu" (MCC, 2/22b–23a). The original poems by Wu Wei-yeh can be found in *Wu Mei-ts'un shih-chi chien-chu* 吳梅村詩集箋注 (Shanghai: Ku-chi ch'u-pan-she, 1983), 1:358–360. These poems by Wu Wei-yeh can be dated by their position in his collected works to 1653–1654. Wu Li also has a poem entitled "Sent to Han-lin Compiler Mei-ts'un [that is, Wu Wei-yeh]," MCC, 2/28b (translated here; see p. 109).

22. MCC, 2/14b–15b.

23. Strassberg, *World of K'ung Shang-jen*, p. 394.

24. MCC, 2/15b–16a.

25. Jonathan Chaves, "The Yellow Mountain Poems of Ch'ien Ch'ien-i (1582–1664): Poetry as *Yu-chi*," *Harvard Journal of Asiatic Studies* 48(2) (Dec. 1988):489. For an excellent account of Ch'ien as a man of letters, with a thorough bibliography of studies of his literary theory, see the entry on him by Ming-shui Hung in William H. Nienhauser, Jr., ed., *The Indiana Companion to Traditional Chinese Literature* (Bloomington: Indiana University Press, 1986), pp. 277–279.

26. Irving Yucheng Lo and William Schultz, eds., *Waiting for the Unicorn:*

*Poems and Lyrics of China's Last Dynasty* (Bloomington: Indiana University Press, 1986), p. 15.

27. Ch'en Yüan, *Nien-p'u*, pp. 6–8.

28. For the three Wang Shih-chen poems, see his *Yü-yang shan-jen chu-shu* 漁洋山人著述 (K'ang-hsi period edition), *Yü-yang hsü chi* 續集, 1/7b and 9b. For the two Shih Jun-chang poems, see his *Shih Yü-shan hsien-sheng ch'üan chi* 施愚山先生全集 (edition of 1765), *shih-chi* 詩集, 46/5b and 48/12b (the second apparently overlooked by Ch'en Yüan). For the Sung Wan poem, see his *An-ya-t'ang shih chi* 安雅堂詩集 (Ch'ing edition in Library of Congress), *wei-k'o kao* 未刻稿, 1/23a. For the Ch'eng K'o-tse poem, see *Ch'eng Huang-chen shih* 程湟榛詩 in Wei Hsien 魏憲 (second half seventeenth century), ed., *Huang Ch'ing pai-ming-chia shih* 皇清百名家詩 (K'ang-hsi period edition, Fu-ch'ing Wei-shih chen-chiang-t'ang 福清魏氏枕江堂), 33/18b. The text of this last poem differs in certain details from the citation in Ch'en Yüan's *Nien-p'u* of Wu Li.

29. Ch'en Yüan, *Nien-p'u*, p. 7.

30. Shih Jun-chang, *Shih Yü-shan . . .* , *wen-chi* 文集, 6/7a–b.

31. James J. Y. Liu, *Chinese Theories of Literature* (Chicago: University of Chicago Press, 1975), p. 45.

32. Lo and Schultz, *Waiting for the Unicorn*, p. 18.

33. See the new edition in four volumes published by the Peking Chung-hua shu-chü, 1986. See also the discussion of the book by J. D. Schmidt in Nienhauser, *Indiana Companion*, pp. 736–738. For a detailed account of the compilers of *Sung-shih ch'ao*, see Yuasa Yukihiko 湯淺幸孫, "Sō-shi shō no senja-tachi—hito ni yotte shi o sonsu" 「宋詩鈔」の選者たち—人によつて史を存す [The compilers of the *Sung-shih ch'ao*: comprehending history through men], *Chūgoku bungaku hō* 中國文學報 20 (1965):68–92.

34. Wu Chih-chen, *Huang-yeh-ts'un-chuang chi* 黃葉邨莊集 (edition of 1878 in Library of Congress), 2/5a–b.

35. For a discussion of *tan*, see Jonathan Chaves, *Mei Yao-ch'en and the Development of Early Sung Poetry* (New York: Columbia University Press, 1976), pp. 114–125.

36. Ou-yang Hsiu, *Liu-i shih-hua*, in Martin, *Index*, p. 158. See the translation in Chaves, *Mei Yao-ch'en*, p. 110.

37. Lo and Schultz, *Waiting for the Unicorn*, pp. 21–22.

38. Wu Chih-chen, *Huang-yeh-ts'un-chuang chi*, 2/10a.

39. Wang Mou-lin, *Pai-ch'ih-wu-t'ung-ko chi* 百尺梧桐閣集 (Shanghai: Ku-chi ch'u-pan-she, 1980; photographic reprint in 3 vols. of K'ang-hsi period edition), 2:868–869.

40. Lo and Schultz, *Waiting for the Unicorn*, pp. 22–26. See also Madeline Chu, "Interplay Between Tradition and Innovation: The Seventeenth Century Tz'u Revival," *Chinese Literature: Essays, Articles, Reviews* 9(1–2) (July 1987):71–88; and David R. McCraw, *Chinese Lyricists of the Seventeenth Century* (Honolulu: University of Hawaii Press, 1990).

41. Wang Mou-lin, *Pai-ch'ih-wu-t'ung-ko chi*, 2:893–894.

42. Liang Ch'ing-piao has a farewell poem addressed to Hsü; see his *Chiao-lin shih-chi* 蕉林詩集 (edition in Library of Congress dated 1678, Ch'iu-pi-t'ang 秋碧堂), *ch'i-yen lü* 七言律, 3/7b. Kung Ting-tzu describes a social gathering at which he and Hsü were both present; see his *Ting-shan-t'ang shih-chi* 定山堂詩集 (1883 reprint of K'ang-hsi edition), 4/28a–b. (The poem on 26/27b is probably another description of the same event.) Kung also wrote a colophon, dated 1662, to a calligraphy by Su Shih in the collection of Hsü Chih-chien in which he describes Hsü as "pure and transcendent, cut off from the vulgar"; see his *Ting-shan-t'ang wen-chi* 文集 (1924 reprint of earlier edition), 6/24a.

43. Liang Ch'ing-piao, *Chiao-lin shih-chi, ch'i-yen ku* 七言古, 1/9a–b.

44. Ch'en Hu, *Ch'üeh-an hsien-sheng shih-ch'ao* 確庵先生詩鈔, appended to Lu Shih-i 陸世儀 (1611–1672), *Fu-t'ing hsien-sheng wen-ch'ao* 桴亭先生文鈔 (the whole book alternatively titled *Lu Ch'en erh hsien-sheng wen-ch'ao* 陸陳二先生文鈔, edition in Library of Congress dated 1870, Ho-fei K'uai-shih 合肥蒯氏), 4/22a.

45. See Jonathan Chaves, "Moral Action in the Poetry of Wu Chia-chi 吳嘉紀 (1618–84)," *Harvard Journal of Asiatic Studies* 46(2) (Dec. 1986):387–469, especially pp. 422–423 and the references in n. 75.

46. Kuei Chuang, *Kuei Chuang chi* 集 (Shanghai: Ku-chi ch'u-pan-she, 1984), 1:157–161. Kuei Chuang wrote poems both to Ch'en Hu and to his colleague Lu Shih-i; see *Kuei Chuang chi*, 1:136 and 145. He also wrote a eulogy on a portrait of Ch'ien Mei-hsien 錢梅仙 dressed in "robes of the Way" (*tao fu* 道服) and with an expression on his face of "resentment at Heaven's drunkenness"; *Kuei Chuang chi*, 2:485. Mei-hsien is Ch'ien Ku 假, a disciple of Ch'en Hu.

47. *Kuei Chuang chi*, 2:589. See the discussion of this episode in Frederic Wakeman, Jr., *The Great Enterprise* (Berkeley: University of California Press, 1985), 2:943, n. 114. Wakeman calls the piece a "satirical epic."

48. Wakeman, *The Great Enterprise*, 2:879, n. 85.

49. Luther Carrington Goodrich, *The Literary Inquisition of Ch'ien-lung* (Baltimore: Waverly Press, 1935), pp. 101–102, 105–106.

50. Ch'ien Ch'ien-i, *Yu-hsüeh chi*, 44/6b–8a.

51. Wakeman, *The Great Enterprise*, 2:1093–1094.

52. Ibid., p. 944, n. 118; p. 1001, n. 30. Wei's poems are anthologized in Shen Te-ch'ien et al., *Ch'ing-shih pieh-ts'ai chi*, 1:59–60; Teng Chih-ch'eng, *Ch'ing-shih chi-shih ch'u-pien*, 2:619–620; and Chang Ying-ch'ang 張應昌 (1790–1874), ed., *Ch'ing-shih to* 清詩鐸 (Peking: Chung-hua shu-chü, 1983; reprint of 1960 edition), 2:552, 758.

53. Jacques Gernet, "Problèmes d'acclimatation du christianisme dans la Chine du XVIIᵉ siècle," in Alain Forest and Yoshiharu Tsuboi, eds., *Catholicisme et Sociétés Asiatiques* (Éditions L'Harmattan/Sophia University, 1988), pp. 38–40.

54. Lu Shih-i, *Fu-t'ing hsien-sheng shih-ch'ao* (see note 44), 3/7b.

55. *Huai-yün wen-ta*, in *Hsiao-shih shan-fang ts'ung-shu*, pp. 5a–b.

56. As translated in William Theodore de Bary et al., *Sources of Chinese Tradition* (New York: Columbia University Press, 1960), p. 482.

57. *Huai-yün wen-ta, hsü-pien* 續編, pp. 10a–b.

58. Ibid., pp. 15aff.

59. *Chung-yung*, 26.9.

60. Ch'ien Ch'ien-i, *Yu-hsüeh chi*, 20/10b–11b.

61. Ch'en Yüan, "Wu Yü-shan," p. 165.

62. Ch'en Hu, *Ch'üeh-an hsien-sheng shih-ch'ao*, 5/22b (two poems); 6/2a–b (two poems), 3a, 3b, 4a; Wu Li, MCC, 2/19a (the central poem is "echoed" by Ch'en at his 5/22b), 19b, 29b (two poems; the central poem on the page echoed by Ch'en Hu at his 6/2a–b), 30a (two poems echoing Ch'en Hu, 6/2b–3a).

63. *Ts'ung-yu chi*, in *Ch'iao-fan-lou ts'ung-shu* 峭帆樓叢書 (1917), *shang* 上 / 33b–35a.

64. A. C. Graham, trans., *The Book of Lieh Tzu* (London: John Murray, 1960), p. 64, n. 1.

65. Yen Ling-feng 嚴靈峰, ed., *Lieh Tzu chang-chü hsin-pien* 列子章句新編 (Taipei: Wu-ch'iu-pei-chai 1960), p. 73; *Wen hsüan* 文選 (Hong Kong: Shang-wu yin-shu-kuan, 1960), 1:27.

66. Graham, *Book of Lieh Tzu*, p. 62.

67. David R. Knechtges, trans. *Wen Xuan*, Vol. 1: *Rhapsodies on Metropolises and Capitals* (Princeton: Princeton University Press, 1982), p. 185.

68. MCC, 3/57b–58a.

69. *Hou Han shu* 後漢書 (Peking: Chung-hua shu-chü, 1982; reprint of 1965 edition in 12 vols.), 8:2299; Lo Kuan-chung 羅貫中 *San-kuo chih yen-i* 三國志演義 (Hong Kong: Shang-wu yin-shu-kuan, 1962), vol. 1, ch. 1, p. 2.

70. For the various legends involving Ts'ang Chieh, see Jonathan Chaves, "The Legacy of Ts'ang Chieh: The Written Word as Magic," *Oriental Art*, n.s., 23(2) (Summer 1977):200–215.

71. Kuei Chuang, *Kuei Chuang chi*, 1:157.

72. Ibid., 2:485.

73. Ch'en Hu, ed., *Ts'ung-yu chi, shang*/33a.

74. See *Kuei Chuang chi*, pp. 58–59.

75. J. C. Yang and T. Numata, entry on Ch'ü Shih-ssu in Hummel, *Eminent Chinese*, pp. 199–201. For a Marxist perspective on Ch'ü as patriotic hero, completely ignoring his Christianity, see *Ch'ü Shih-ssu chi* 集, prepared by the Department of History of Chiang-su Normal College and the Chiang-su Regional History Research Institute (Shanghai: Ku-chi ch'u-pan-she, 1981), foreword, pp. 1–4.

76. Lu Shih-i, *Fu-t'ing hsien-sheng shih-ch'ao*, 7/14a–b.

77. *Shih-yung fo-hsüeh tz'u-tien* 實用佛學辭典 (Hong Kong: Fo-ching liu-

t'ung-ch'u, 1959 reprint), 2:1395–1396. See the translation by Leon Hurvitz, *Scripture of the Lotus Blossom of the Fine Dharma* (New York: Columbia University Press, 1976), p. 30.

78. P'an Lei, *Sui-ch'u-t'ang chi* 遂初堂集 (edition dated 1710 in Library of Congress), *Shao-yu ts'ao* 少遊草, *shang*/9a.

79. Ch'en Hu, *Ch'üeh-an hsien-sheng shih-ch'ao*, 6/22b.

80. Ch'en Hu, *Ch'üeh-an hsien-sheng wen-chi*, 3/39a–40a.

81. Ch'en Hu, *Ch'üeh-an wen-kao* 確庵文藁, edited by Sun Yen 孫岩, pp. 21a–b (the MS is unpaginated).

82. Ibid., p. 12a.

83. *Huai-yün wen-ta, hsü-pien*, pp. 32a–33b.

84. See Teng Chih-ch'eng, *Ch'ing-shih chi-shih*, 1:59.

85. Ch'ü Ta-chün, *Weng-shan wen-wai* 翁山文外 (edition dated 1920, Wu-hsing Liu-shih Chia-yeh-t'ang 吳興劉氏嘉業堂), 5/2b–3b. See also the account in Hummel, *Eminent Chinese*, p. 201.

86. Gernet, "Problèmes d'acclimatation," p. 45.

87. David E. Mungello, "The Seventeenth-Century Jesuit Translation Project of the Confucian Four Books," in Charles E. Ronan, S.J., and Bonnie B. C. Oh, eds., *East Meets West: The Jesuits in China, 1582–1773* (Chicago: Loyola University Press, 1988), p. 266. See also Mungello's *Curious Land: Jesuit Accommodation and the Origins of Sinology* (Honolulu: University of Hawaii Press, 1989).

88. Wakeman, *The Great Enterprise*, 2:1082, n. 19; 1084, n. 25. See also Lynne A. Struve, "Ambivalence and Action: Some Frustrated Scholars of the K'ang-hsi Period," in Jonathan D. Spence and John E. Wills, Jr., eds., *From Ming to Ch'ing: Conquest, Region, and Continuity in Seventeenth-Century China* (New Haven and London: Yale University Press, 1979), pp. 321–365.

89. Lin Xiaoping, "Wu Li's Religious Belief and *A Lake in Spring*," in *Archives of Asian Art* 40 (1987):29.

90. Ibid., p. 32. For the poem by Wu Li, see Fang Hao, ed., "Wu Yü-shan hsien-sheng 'San-yü chi' chiao-shih," 吳漁山先生「三餘集」校釋 as reprinted in CKH, pp. 101–102.

91. Lin Xiaoping, "Wu Li's Religious Belief," pp. 33–34.

92. See Wu Chih-chen, *Huang-yeh-ts'un-chuang chi*, opposite p. 1a of preface.

93. Lu Lung-chi, *Lu Tzu ch'üan shu* 陸子全書 (K'ang-hsi period edition in Library of Congress), *jih-chi* 日記, 3/10a.

94. Lu Lung-chi, *jih-chi*, 3/13b.

95. For more on this theory, see Jonathan Chaves, "'Not the Way of Poetry': The Poetics of Experience in the Sung Dynasty," *Chinese Literature: Essays, Articles, Reviews* 4(2) (July 1982):199–212.

96. Willard J. Peterson, "Why Did They Become Christians?—Yang T'ing-yün, Li Chih-tsao, and Hsü Kuang-ch'i," in Ronan and Oh, *East Meets West*, p. 129. For Yang T'ing-yün, see also Nicholas Standaert, *Yang Tingyun, Confucian and Christian in Late Ming China* (Leiden: E. J. Brill, 1987), and the

reviews of this book by John W. Witek, S.J., in *Theological Studies* 50(2) ( June 1989):369–371; and myself, in *Crisis* 8(2) (Feb. 1990):55–56. For the relationship between Confucianism and Christianity in general, see Julia Ching, *Confucianism and Christianity: A Comparative Study* (Tokyo: Kodansha, 1977); and Hans Küng and Julia Ching, *Christianity and Chinese Religions* (New York: Doubleday, 1989). Also valuable for the problem of whether certain Confucian practices were idolatrous is George Minamiki, S.J., *The Chinese Rites Controversy* (Chicago: Loyola University Press, 1985).

97. Peterson, "Why Did They Become Christians?", pp. 134–136.

98. For the MS in Wu Li's own calligraphy, see Tam, catalog item 36, p. 355. For a printed version with annotations, see Fang Hao, "*San-yü chi*," p. 88. For Ch'en Yüan's discussion of the matter, see his *Nien-p'u* of Wu Li, p. 17. On p. 16, T'ang Pin's measures are described in some detail.

99. See the entry on T'ang in Hummel, *Eminent Chinese*, pp. 709–710; Shen Te-ch'ien et al., *Ch'ing-shih pieh-ts'ai chi*, 1:107–108; Teng Chih-ch'eng, *Ch'ing-shih chi-shih*, 2:905–906. See also Strassberg, *The World of K'ung Shang-jen*, pp. 120–121, 352–353.

100. T'ang Pin, *T'ang Tzu i-shu* 湯子遺書 (edition of 1870 in Library of Congress), *Chiang-nan kung-tu* 江南公牘, 9/38b–39a.

101. For Lü Liu-liang, see his *Lü Wan-ts'un hsien-sheng shih wen chi* 呂晚村先生詩文集 (edition of 1869 in Library of Congress), 1/20a–21b. For Wang Shih-chen, see his *Ch'ih-pei ou-t'an* 池北偶談 (Peking: Chung-hua shu-chü, 1982), 1:79–80. For Yu T'ung, see his *Yu T'ai-shih hsi-t'ang yü-chi* 尤太史西堂餘集 (edition of 1694 in Library of Congress), *Ken-chai chüan-kao* 艮齋倦稿, *wen* 文, 1/10b–13b (especially p. 12a). For Lu Lung-chi, see his diary entry for the twenty-third day of the intercalary month (after the fourth) for the year *ping-yin* 丙寅 ( June 13, 1686), in his *jih-chi* (see note 93 above), 9/14b.

102. Wang Shih-chen, *Ch'ih-pei ou-t'an*, 1:79–80.

103. T'ang Pin, *T'ang Tzu i-shu*, *Chiang-hsi kung-tu* 江西公牘, 8/9a–10b.

104. T'ang Shao-tsu 唐紹祖 et al., comp., *Ta Ch'ing lü-li* 大清律例, 16/6a.

105. Gernet, "Problèmes d'acclimatation," p. 40.

106. Ch'en Yüan, *Nien-p'u*, p. 17.

107. Fang Hao, "'*San-yü chi*'," p. 89.

108. Ch'en Yüan, "Wu Yü-shan chih Ch'an yu," 吳漁山之禪友 in *Ch'en Yüan shih-hsüeh lun-chu hsüan*, pp. 405–408. For another painting by Wu Li dedicated to Mo-jung and bearing inscriptions by Wang Shih-min, Hsü Chih-chien, and Wu Wei-yeh, see note 21.

109. P'ang Yüan-chi, *Hsü-chai ming-hua lu* (1909), 14/"Wu Yü-shan," pp. 1aff.

110. Ibid., pp. 3a–b.

111. The first form of the title was apparently adopted by Li Ti, the editor of MCC, where the text constitutes ch. 5. The second form is given by Albert Chan, S.J., in his article, "Late Ming Society and the Jesuit Missionaries," in

Ronan and Oh, *East Meets West*, p. 171. The third form is given by Louis Pfister, S.J. (1833–1891), *Notices Biographiques et Bibliographiques sur les Jésuites de l'Ancienne Mission de Chine*, vol. 1 (Kraus reprint, 1971, of 1932 Shanghai publication), p. 396.

112. See Pfister, *Notices*, p. 396; and MCC, 5/80b.

113. For Yeh, see L. Carrington Goodrich and Chaoying Fang, eds., *Dictionary of Ming Biography* (New York: Columbia University Press, 1976), 2:1567–1570.

114. MCC, 5/94a–b.

115. G. K. Chesterton, "The Dagger with Wings" (1926), in *The Complete Father Brown* (Harmondsworth: Penguin Books, 1981), p. 418. For a recent study of the *yü-lu* format, see Daniel K. Gardner, "Modes of Thinking and Modes of Discourse in the Sung: Some Thoughts on the *Yü-lu* ('Recorded Conversations') Texts," *Journal of Asian Studies* 50(3) (Aug. 1991):574–603.

116. MCC, 5/76b.

117. MCC, 3/53b–54a, 54b–57a.

118. MCC, 3/61a.

119. Feifel renders this line, "The old record (O.T.) once spoke of fidelity, wisdom, justification." See Ch'en Yüan, "Wu Yü-shan," p. 167. It seems more likely that Wu Li has in mind here a classic Confucian text such as the *Ta hsüeh* 大學 in which *ch'eng* 誠, *ming* 明, and *shan* 善 all appear.

120. *Han shu* (Peking: Chung-hua shu-chü, 1983; reprint of 1962 edition in 12 vols.), 4:964.

121. See Kenneth J. DeWoskin, *A Song for One or Two: Music and the Concept of Art in Early China* (Ann Arbor: Center for Chinese Studies, University of Michigan, 1982), p. 46.

122. See Fung Yu-lan, *A History of Chinese Philosophy* (Princeton: Princeton University Press, 1953), 2:434ff.

123. Thomas Molnar, *The Pagan Temptation* (Grand Rapids: William B. Eerdmans, 1987), pp. 44–45.

124. Lin Xiaoping, "Wu Li's Religious Belief," pp. 24–25. See also Ch'en Yüan, *Nien-p'u*, p. 12 top.

125. Ch'en Wei-sung, *Chia-ling ch'üan chi* 迦陵全集 (K'ang-hsi period edition in Library of Congress), *Chia-ling tz'u ch'üan chi*, 12/4b. See Ch'en Yüan, *Nien-p'u*, p. 12; Lin Xiaoping, "Wu Li's Religious Belief," p. 29. For Ch'en's role in the *tz'u* revival, see Chu, "Interplay," and McCraw, *Chinese Lyricists*, pp. 63–86. For Rougemont, see also George H. Dunne, S.J., *Generation of Giants* (Notre Dame: University of Notre Dame Press, 1962), pp. 174, 348, 352. For more on Couplet, see Jerome Heyndrickx, ed., *Philippe Couplet, S.J. (1623–1693)—The Man Who Brought China to Europe* (Nettetal: Steyler Verlag, 1990).

126. Vincent Cronin, *The Wise Man from the West* (London: Readers Union, Rupert Hart-Davis, 1956).

127. MCC, 5/89b.

128. For a useful account of the scientific teachings of the Jesuits, see Willard J. Peterson, "Western Natural Philosophy Published in Late Ming China," *Proceedings of the American Philosophical Society* 117(4) (Aug. 1973):295–322.

129. The poems will be found in MCC, 5/96b and 2/32a.

130. See Fang Hao, "Wu Yü-shan hsien-sheng *'San-pa chi'* chiao-shih," 吳漁山先生「三巴集」校釋, in CKH, pp. 103–116; Wang Tsung-yen's further annotations to these poems in CKH, pp. 141–146; and the *San-yü chi* with annotations by Fang Hao in CKH, pp. 85–102. Li I-kang 李毅剛 (under the name "I-kang") has recently published an anthology of poems about Macao entitled *Ao-men ssu-pai nien shih hsüan* 澳門四百年詩選 (Macao: Ao-men ch'u-pan-she, 1990). This anthology presents two of Wu Li's poems on Macao, as well as one by Ch'ü Ta-chün (pp. 12–16). The only earlier poems on the subject given by Li I-kang are a group of four by T'ang Hsien-tsu 湯顯祖 (1550–1616), four by the Buddhist monk Chi-shan 跡刪 (b. 1577)—which have also been called to my attention by Pei-yi Wu—and one by a certain Chang Mu 張穆 (1606–1687), pp. 3–12. Incredibly, Li accepts without question as historical fact the rumor of Wu Li's trip to the West, "several tens of thousands of *li* away" (p. 13).

131. Pfister, *Notices*, p. 396.

132. See the reprint in CKH, pp. 69–84. The publishing history is given on p. 84; Fang's own account of how he discovered the MS is on p. 86.

133. I have discussed elsewhere the equivocal reputation of such poems in the traditional Chinese critical literature: see Jonathan Chaves, "'Meaning Beyond the Painting'—the Chinese Painter as Poet," in Alfreda Murck and Wen Fong, eds., *Words and Images: Chinese Poetry, Calligraphy, and Painting* (New York: Metropolitan Museum of Art and Princeton University Press, 1991).

134. MCC, 3/49b. I follow Fang Hao's emendation of *chi chiu* 計久 to *hsü ting* 許定; see CKH, p. 114. Pfister's claim—derived from "a little *Life* in MS of this saintly man written in Chinese in the last century"—that Wu attempted to burn all his preconversion poems and paintings seems inadequately founded and may in fact have been based on a misreading of the very poem translated here. See Pfister, *Notices*, p. 396.

135. MCC, 3/42a–43a.

136. See also Yu T'ung, *Yu T'ai-shih hsi-t'ang yü-chi, Ken-chai chüan-kao, wen,* 7/6a–b. Clara Yü Cuadrado gives a good account of Yu as a literary figure, with bibliography, in her entry on him in Nienhauser, *Indiana Companion*, pp. 939–940.

137. For Yu T'ung's assignment as assistant compiler of the *Ming History*, see the entry on him in Hummel, *Eminent Chinese*, pp. 935–936.

138. For Yu T'ung's "Bamboo Branch Songs on Foreign Countries," see the complete set in Yu T'ung, *Hsi-t'ang ch'üan chi* 西堂全集 (K'ang-hsi period edition in Library of Congress).

139. This alludes to Yang Hsiung 揚雄 (53 B.C.–A.D. 18), the putative au-

thor of a book called *Fang yen* 方言, "Languages of the Localities." The expression *chi yu su* 齎油素 comes from Yang's letter to Liu Hsin 劉歆, in which he writes, "I have often taken my little three-inch brush, *prepared writing silk four feet in length*, and gone off to inquire about different languages [or dialects]" (emphasis added). The passage is cited under "*yu su*" in Morohashi Tetsuji 諸橋轍次, *Daikanwa jiten* 大漢和辭典 (Tokyo: Taishūkan shōten, 1957–1960), 12:13568, col. 2.

140. Ch'en Yüan, *Nien-p'u*, p. 17.

141. For Yu T'ung's poems on France and Holland, see his "Bamboo Branch Songs on Foreign Countries" (see note 138), pp. 11b and 12a.

142. Yen Ling-fen, pp. 72–73; Graham, *Book of Lieh Tzu*, pp. 61–62. (See notes 64 and 65.)

143. Francis A. Rouleau, S.J., "The First Chinese Priest of the Society of Jesus—Emmanuel de Siqueira (1633–73)," *Archivum Historicum Societatis Iesu* 28 (1959):3–50. The entire account of de Siqueira is based on this article. For Couplet's acquaintanceship with him (or with his story), see p. 16, n. 38. See also George H. Dunne, *Generation of Giants*, p. 174. Wu Li's own baptismal name was Simon-Xavier a Cunha. Recent research has demonstrated that Wu Li was one of five men initially chosen to accompany Couplet to Rome, but the newly appointed Jesuit vice-provincial in China, Giandomenico Gabiani, forbade Wu Li to take the trip on the grounds of his relative old age. Only one Chinese convert, a certain Shen Fu-tsung 沈福宗, or Michael Shen, ended up going all the way to Europe with Couplet. While there, Shen and Couplet would have audiences with Louis XIV of France, James II of England, and Pope Innocent XI. For these facts, see the relevant comments by Albert Chan, S.J., and Theodore Nicholas Foss in Jerome Heyndrickx, ed., *Philippe Couplet, S.J. (1623–1693)—the Man Who Brought China to Europe* (Nettetal: Steyler Verlag, 1990), pp. 71–72, 75, 122–123, 126–127; and Foss's entire contribution, "The European Sojourn of Philippe Couplet and Michael Shen Fuzong—1683–1692," pp. 121–142. As Albert Chan suggests, Couplet may have been introduced to Wu Li by de Rougemont and may well have served as Wu Li's spiritual director. See Chan's essay in the Heyndrickx volume, "Towards a Chinese Church: The Contribution of Philippe Couplet, S.J.," p. 72n. Given such a relationship, Couplet may eventually be shown to have been the man who actually baptized Wu Li. (I am indebted to John Witek, S.J., for his suggestion of this possibility.)

144. Jonathan Spence, *The Question of Hu* (New York: Alfred A. Knopf, 1988).

145. See Jonathan Chaves, "Yellow Mountain Poems," pp. 475–476 and passim.

146. C. R. Boxer, "Macao Three Hundred Years Ago, as Described by Antonio Bocarro in 1635," *T'ien Hsia Monthly* 6(4) (April 1938):281–316. The following account of Macao is based on this article.

147. Ch'ü Ta-chün, *Weng-shan shih-wai* 翁山詩外 (edition dated 1910,

Shanghai Kuo-hsüeh fu-lun-she), 9/32b–33a. The poems in this work are arranged chronologically. On pp. 5b–6a is found a poem on New Year's day, the year *wu-ch'en* 戊辰 (1688); this poem contains the line, "Next year I will be sixty [*sui:* fifty-nine by Western reckoning]." Ch'ü was born in 1630. The Macao poems are followed closely (on pp. 33a–b) by a poem dating from the last month of *chi-ssu* 己巳, or 1689.

148. Ch'ü Ta-chün, *Kuang-tung hsin-yü* 廣東新語 (Hong Kong: Chung-hua shu-chü, 1974), pp. 36–38.

149. See Fang Hao, "'*San-yü chi*,'" p. 102. For Wu Li's holograph see Tam, *Six Masters*, p. 361.

150. MCC, 2/38a–b.

151. Tomioka Masutarō 富岡益太郎, *Shi-Ō Go Un* 四王吳惲 (Osaka: Hakubundō, 1919), pl. 32.

152. John N. Wall, Jr., ed., *George Herbert: The Country Parson, The Temple* (New York: Paulist Press, Classics of Western Spirituality, 1981), pp. 284–285.

153. Ibid., pp. 278–279.

154. C. S. Lewis, *Surprised by Joy: The Shape of My Early Life* (San Diego: Harcourt Brace Jovanovich, n.d., Harvest Books edition of 1955 publication), p. 56.

155. MCC, 3/53a–b.

156. MCC, 3/57a–58b and 59a–61a.

157. *Holy Image, Holy Space: Icons and Frescoes from Greece* (Greek Ministry of Culture, Byzantine Museum of Athens, and Walters Art Gallery, Baltimore, 1988); see the illustration on p. 156 and the entry by Myrtali Acheimastou-Potamianou, pp. 224–227.

158. Gernet, *China and the Christian Impact*, p. 223.

159. *Li Sao*, in *Wen Hsüan*, 2:718.

160. David Hawkes, *The Songs of the South* (Harmondsworth: Penguin Books, 1985), p. 74.

161. *Ch'u tz'u pu-chu* 楚辭補注 (in Ssu-pu pei-yao), 17/12b.

162. Hawkes, *Songs of the South*, p. 315.

163. Mircea Eliade, *Shamanism: Archaic Techniques of Ecstasy* (Princeton: Princeton University Press, Bollingen Series, 1964), pp. 487–494.

164. Ibid., p. 489.

165. Joseph P. Smith, S.J., trans., *St. Irenaeus: Proof of the Apostolic Preaching* (New York and Ramsey: Newman Press, 1952), p. 77.

166. See the English translation by Colm Luibheid and Norman Russell in the Classics of Western Spirituality series (New York: Paulist Press, 1982).

167. Ibid., introduction by Bishop Kallistos Ware, pp. 67–68.

168. C. J. deCatanzaro, trans., *St. Symeon the New Theologian: The Discourses* (New York: Paulist Press, Classics of Western Spirituality, 1980), p. 333. For illustrations of the *Ladder*, see J. R. Martin, *The Illustration of the Heavenly Ladder of John Climacus* (Princeton: Princeton University Press, 1974).

169. Anne Ridder, ed., *Thomas Traherne: Poems, Centuries and Three Thanksgivings* (London: Oxford University Press, 1966), p. 191.

170. For a good color photograph of the façade, see *Free China Review* 40(3) (March 1990):54–55.

171. Karlgren, *Book of Odes*, pp. 185–187.

172. Waley, *Book of Songs*, p. 250.

173. Su Shih, *Tung-p'o chi* 東坡集, in *Tung-p'o ch'i-chi* 七集 (in Ssu-pu pei-yao), 1/1a.

174. Gernet, *China and the Christian Impact*, pp. 142, 277–278, n. 8.

175. D. C. Lau, trans., *Confucius: The Analects* (Harmondsworth: Penguin Books, 1979), p. 112.

176. *Honan Ch'eng-shih i-shu* 河南程氏遺書 (edition of 1871 in Library of Congress; Nanking: Liu-an-ch'iu-wo-chai 六安求我齋), *wen-chi* 文集, 8/10b–11b.

177. See *Ishikawa Jōzan hitsuboku* 石川丈山筆墨 (Kyoto Mingcikan [Kyoto Folk Art Museum], 1974), pp. 18–20.

178. MCC, 3/61b–62b.

179. John Eudes Bamberger, O.C.S.O., trans., *Evagrius Ponticus: The Praktikos; Chapters on Prayer* (Kalamazoo: Cistercian Publications, 1981), p. 20.

180. Colm Luibheid, trans., *John Cassian: Conferences* (New York and Mahwah: Paulist Press, Classics of Western Spirituality, 1985), pp. 134–135.

181. See CKH, p. 69. The manual in question would have been an incomplete translation of the Roman Missal by Buglio, published in Peking in 1670. See Albert Chan, S.J., "Towards a Chinese Church," in Jerome Heyndrickx, ed., *Philippe Couplet*, pp. 73–74. Of course, future research may well reveal that certain phrases in other of Wu Li's religious poems may have derived from Jesuit translations of Catholic literature. At the same time, it should be kept in mind that Wu Li knew Latin, and indeed the very first poem in the sequence of *ch'ü* on the mass includes the line, "The rituals are annotated in Western Ch'in," where "Western Ch'in," if Fang Hao is right, means "Latin" (see CKH, p. 69). Wu Li may have mined the Jesuit translations for certain phrases in his Chinese poems, while employing the original Latin in the actual performance of the mass and in consulting the Missal itself.

182. CKH, pp. 70–71. I am indebted to John Witek, S.J., for his help with this poem as well as for many valuable suggestions and references.

183. CKH, p. 73.

184. CKH, pp. 76, 79.

185. CKH, pp. 80ff.

186. CKH, p. 81.

187. *Fang Hao liu-shih tzu-ting-kao* 方豪六十自定稿 (Taipei: Ching-yin shu-kuan, 1969), 2:1626. I am indebted to Albert Chan, S.J., for this and other references.

188. Personal communication, July 11, 1989. See Chan's related comments in the *New Catholic Encyclopedia* (see note 7).

# Bibliography

Bamberger, John Eudes, O.C.S.O., trans. *Evagrius Ponticus: The Praktikos; Chapters on Prayer*. Kalamazoo: Cistercian Publications, 1981.

Boxer, C. R. "Macao Three Hundred Years Ago, As Described by Antonio Bocarro in 1635." *T'ien Hsia Monthly* 6(4) (April 1938):281–316.

Chan, Albert, S.J. "Late Ming Society and the Jesuit Missionaries." In Ronan and Oh, pp. 153–172.

Chang Feng-chen 張奉箴. *"Ch'ing-ch'u liu ta hua-chia chih i ye-su hui-shih wu yü-shan,"* 清初六大畫家之一耶穌會士吳漁山. *Kao-hsiung shih-ta hsüeh-pao* 高雄師大學報, 1991, #2, pp. 117–157.

Chang Ying-ch'ang 張應昌 (1790–1874), ed. *Ch'ing-shih to* 清詩鐸. Peking: Chung-hua shu-chü, 1983; reprint of 1960 ed., 2 vols.

Chaves, Jonathan. "The Legacy of Ts'ang Chieh: The Written Word as Magic." *Oriental Art*, n.s., 23(2) (Summer 1977):200–215.

————. "'Meaning Beyond the Painting'—the Chinese Painter as Poet." In Alfreda Murck and Wen Fong, eds., *Words and Images: Chinese Poetry, Calligraphy, and Painting* (New York: Metropolitan Museum of Art and Princeton University Press, 1991).

————. *Mei Yao-ch'en and the Development of Early Sung Poetry*. New York: Columbia University Press, 1976.

————. "Moral Action in the Poetry of Wu Chia-chi (1618–84)." *Harvard Journal of Asiatic Studies* 46(2) (Dec. 1986):387–469.

————. "'Not the Way of Poetry:' The Poetics of Experience in the Sung Dynasty." *Chinese Literature: Essays, Articles, Reviews* 4(2) (July 1982):199–212.

————. Review of Nicholas Standaert, *Yang Tingyun*. *Crisis* 8(2) (Feb. 1990):55–56.

————. "The Yellow Mountain Poems of Ch'ien Ch'ien-i (1582–1664): Poetry as *Yu-chi*." *Harvard Journal of Asiatic Studies* 48(2) (Dec. 1988): 465–492.

Ch'en Hu 陳瑚. *Ch'üeh-an hsien-sheng shih-ch'ao* 確庵先生詩鈔. Appended to Lu Shih-i, *Fu-t'ing hsien-sheng wen-ch'ao*.

————. *Ch'üeh-an wen-kao* 確庵文蒿. Edited by Sun Yen 孫岩. Unpaginated MS in Library of Congress.

————, ed. *Ts'ung-yu chi* 從游集. In *Ch'iao-fan-lou ts'ung-shu* 峭帆樓叢書 (1917).

Ch'en Wei-sung 陳維崧. *Chia-ling ch'üan chi* 迦陵全集. K'ang-hsi period edition in Library of Congress.

Ch'en Yü-chi 陳玉琪. *Hsüeh-wen-t'ang wen-chi* 學文堂文集. In *Ch'ang-chou hsien-che i-shu* 常州先哲遺書 (preface dated 1686).

Ch'en Yüan 陳垣. *Ch'en Yüan hsüeh-shu lun-wen chi, ti erh chi* 陳垣學術論文集, 第二集. Peking: Chung-hua shu-chü, 1982.

————. *Ch'en Yüan hsüeh-shu lun-wen chi, ti i chi* 第一集. Peking: Chung-hua shu-chü, 1980.

————. *Ch'en Yüan shih-hsüeh lun-chu hsüan* 史學論著選. Shanghai: Jen-min ch'u-pan-she, 1981.

————. "Wu Yü-shan—in Commemoration of the 250th Anniversary of His Ordination to the Priesthood in the Society of Jesus." Translated by Eugene Feifel. *Monumenta Serica* 3 (1938):130–170.

Ch'eng I. See under *Honan Ch'eng-shih i-shu.*

Ch'eng K'o-tse 程可則. *Ch'eng Huang-chen shih* 程湟榛詩. In Wei Hsien, *Huang Ch'ing pai-ming-chia shih.*

Chesterton, G. K. *The Complete Father Brown.* Harmondsworth: Penguin Books, 1981.

Ch'ien Ch'ien-i 錢謙益. *Yu-hsüeh chi* 有學集. Sui-Han-chai 邃漢齋 edition dated 1910.

Ching, Julia. *Confucianism and Christianity: A Comparative Study.* Tokyo: Kodansha, 1977.

Chou K'ang-hsieh 周康燮, ed. *Wu Yü-shan yen-chiu lun-chi* 吳漁山研究論集. Hong Kong: Ch'ung-wen Bookstore, 1971.

Chu I-tsun 朱彝尊. *Ming-shih tsung* 明詩綜. Taipei: Shih-chieh shu-chü; reprint of 1962, 2 vols.

Chu, Madeline. "Interplay Between Tradition and Innovation: The Seventeenth Century Tz'u Revival." *Chinese Literature: Essays, Articles, Reviews* 9(1–2) (July 1987):71–88.

*Ch'u tz'u pu-chu* 楚辭補注. In Ssu-pu pei-yao.

Ch'ü Shih-ssu 瞿式耜. *Ch'ü Shih-ssu chi* 集. Prepared by the Department of History of Chiang-su Normal College and the Chiang-su Regional History Research Institute. Shanghai: Ku-chi ch'u-pan-she, 1981.

Ch'ü Ta-chün 屈大均. *Kuang-tung hsin-yü* 廣東新語. Hong Kong: Chung-hua shu-chü, 1974.

————. *Weng-shan shih-wai* 翁山詩外. Shanghai: Kuo-hsüeh fu-lun-she, 1910.

————. *Weng-shan wen-wai* 文外. Wu-hsing Liu-shih Chia-yeh-t'ang 吳興劉氏嘉業堂, 1920.

Ch'ung I 崇彝. *Hsüan-hsüeh-chai shu hua yü-mu chi* 選學齋書畫寓目記. 1921; on microfilm in Freer-Sackler Library, Washington, D.C.

Cronin, Vincent. *The Wise Man from the West.* London: Readers Union, Rupert Hart-Davis, 1956.

de Bary, William Theodore, et al. *Sources of Chinese Tradition.* New York: Columbia University Press, 1960.

deCatanzaro, C. J., trans. *St. Symeon the New Theologian: The Discourses.* New York: Paulist Press, Classics of Western Spirituality, 1980.

DeWoskin, Kenneth J. *A Song for One or Two: Music and the Concept of Art in Early China.* Ann Arbor: Center for Chinese Studies, University of Michigan, 1982.

Dunne, George H., S.J. *Generation of Giants.* Notre Dame: University of Notre Dame Press, 1962.

Eliade, Mircea. *Shamanism: Archaic Techniques of Ecstasy.* Translated by Willard Trask. Princeton: Princeton University Press, Bollingen Series, 1964.

Fang Hao 方豪. *Fang Hao liu-shih tzu-ting-kao* 方豪六十自定稿. 2 vols. Taipei: Ching-yin shu-kuan, 1969.

———, ed. "*Wu Yü-shan hsien-sheng 'San-pa chi' chiao-shih*" 吳漁山先生「三巴集」校釋. In Chou K'ang-hsieh pp. 103–116.

———, ed. "*Wu Yü-shan hsien-sheng 'San-yü chi' chiao-shih*" 「三餘集」校釋. In Chou K'ang-hsieh, pp. 85–102.

Fung Yu-lan. *A History of Chinese Philosophy.* Vol. 2. Translated by Derk Bodde. Princeton: Princeton University Press, 1953.

Gardner, Daniel K. "Modes of Thinking and Modes of Discourse in the Sung: Some Thoughts on the *Yü-lu* ('Recorded Conversations') Texts." *Journal of Asian Studies* 50(3) (Aug. 1991):574–603.

Gernet, Jacques. *China and the Christian Impact—a Conflict of Cultures.* Cambridge: Cambridge University Press, 1982.

———. "Problèmes d'acclimatation du christianisme dans la Chine du XVIIᵉ siècle." In Alain Forest and Yoshiharu Tsuboi, eds., *Catholicisme et Sociétés Asiatiques.* Éditions L'Harmattan/Sophia University, 1988.

Goodrich, Luther Carrington. *The Literary Inquisition of Ch'ien-lung.* Baltimore: Waverly Press, 1935.

Goodrich, Luther Carrington, and Chaoying Fang, eds. *Dictionary of Ming Biography.* 2 vols. New York: Columbia University Press, 1976.

Graham, A. C., trans. *The Book of Lieh Tzu.* London: John Murray, 1960.

*Han Shu* 漢書. Peking: Chung-hua shu-chü, 1983; reprint of 1962 edition, 12 vols.

Hawkes, David. *The Songs of the South.* Harmondsworth: Penguin Books, 1985.

Herbert, George. See Wall, John N., Jr.

Heyndrickx, Jerome, ed. *Philippe Couplet, S.J. (1623–1693)—The Man Who Brought China to Europe.* Monumenta Serica Monograph Series 22. Nettetal: Steyler Verlag, 1990.

*Holy Image, Holy Space: Icons and Frescoes from Greece.* Catalog of exhibition organized by Greek Ministry of Culture, Byzantine Museum of Athens, and Walters Art Gallery, Baltimore, 1988.

*Honan Ch'eng-shih i-shu* 河南程氏遺書. Nanking: Liu-an-ch'iu-wo-chai 六安求我齋, 1871.

*Hou Han shu* 後漢書. Peking: Chung-hua shu-chü, 1982; reprint of 1965 edition, 12 vols.

*Huai-yün wen-ta* 淮雲問答. In Ku Hsiang.

Hummel, Arthur W., ed. *Eminent Chinese of the Ch'ing Period*. Taipei: Ch'eng-wen Publishing Co., 1975; reprint of 1943 publication.

Hurvitz, Leon, trans. *Scripture of the Lotus Blossom of the Fine Dharma*. New York: Columbia University Press, 1976.

*Ishikawa Jōzan hitsuboku* 石川丈山筆墨. Kyoto: Kyoto Mingeikan [Kyoto Folk Art Museum], 1974.

Karlgren, Bernhard. *The Book of Odes*. Stockholm: Museum of Far Eastern Antiquities, 1950.

Knechtges, David R., trans. *Wen Xuan*, Vol. 1: *Rhapsodies on Metropolises and Capitals*. Princeton: Princeton University Press, 1982.

Ku Hsiang 顧湘, ed. *Hsiao-shih shan-fang ts'ung-shu* 小石山房叢書. 1874.

Ku Wen-pin 顧文彬 (1811–1889). *Kuo-yün-lou shu hua chi* 過雲樓書畫記. 1882. Copy in Freer-Sackler Library.

Kuei Chuang 歸莊. *Kuei Chuang chi* 集. 2 vols. Shanghai: Ku-chi ch'u-pan-she, 1984.

Küng, Hans, and Julia Ching. *Christianity and Chinese Religions*. New York: Doubleday, 1989.

Kung Ting-tzu 龔鼎孳. *Ting-shan-t'ang shih-chi* 定山堂詩集. 1883 reprint of K'ang-hsi edition.

———. *Ting-shan-t'ang wen-chi* 文集. 1924 reprint of earlier edition.

Lau, D. C., trans. *Confucius: The Analects*. Harmondsworth: Penguin Books, 1979.

Lewis, C. S. *Surprised by Joy: The Shape of My Early Life*. San Diego: Harcourt Brace Jovanovich, n.d., Harvest Books edition of 1955 publication.

[Li] I-kang [李] 毅剛. *Ao-men ssu-pai nien shih hsüan* 澳門四百年詩選. Macao: Ao-men ch'u-pan-she, 1990.

Li Ti, S.J. 李杕, ed. *Mo-ching chi* 墨井集. Shanghai: Hsü-chia-wei ("Zikawei") Press, 1909. Copy in East Asian Library at Washington University in St. Louis.

Liang Ch'ing-piao 梁清標. *Chiao-lin shih-chi* 蕉林詩集. Ch'iu-pi-t'ang 秋碧堂, 1678.

Lin Xiaoping. "Wu Li's Religious Belief and *A Lake in Spring*." *Archives of Asian Art* 40 (1987):24–35.

Liu, James J. Y. *Chinese Theories of Literature*. Chicago: University of Chicago Press, 1975.

Lo, Irving Yucheng, and William Schultz, eds. *Waiting for the Unicorn: Poems and Lyrics of China's Last Dynasty*. Bloomington: Indiana University Press, 1986.

Lo Kuan-chung 羅貫中. *San-kuo chih yen-i* 三國志演義. 2 vols. Hong Kong: Shang-wu yin-shu-kuan, 1962.

Lu Lung-chi [or -ch'i] 陸隴其. *Lu Tzu ch'üan shu* 陸子全書. K'ang-hsi period edition in Library of Congress.

Lu Shih-i 陸世儀. *Fu-t'ing hsien-sheng wen-ch'ao* 桴亭先生文鈔. Alternatively titled, *Lu Ch'en erh hsien-sheng wen-ch'ao* 陸陳二先生文鈔 (see Ch'en Hu above). Ho-fei K'uai-shih 合肥劊氏 edition dated 1870.

Lü Liu-liang 呂留良. *Lü Wan-ts'un hsien-sheng shih wen chi* 呂晚村先生詩文集. Edition of 1869 in Library of Congress.

Luibheid, Colm, trans. *John Cassian: Conferences*. New York and Mahwah: Paulist Press, Classics of Western Spirituality, 1985.

Luibheid, Colm, and Norman Russell, trans. *John Climacus: The Ladder of Divine Ascent*. New York: Paulist Press, Classics of Western Spirituality, 1982.

Martin, Helmut, comp. *Index to the Ho Collection of Twenty-Eight Shih-hua with a Punctuated Edition of the Ho Collection of Twenty-Eight Shih-hua*. 2 vols. Taipei: Chinese Materials and Research Aids Service Center, 1973.

Martin, J. R. *The Illustration of the Heavenly Ladder of John Climacus*. Princeton: Princeton University Press, 1974.

McCraw, David R. *Chinese Lyricists of the Seventeenth Century*. Honolulu: University of Hawaii Press, 1990.

Minamiki, George, S.J. *The Chinese Rites Controversy*. Chicago: Loyola University Press, 1985.

Molnar, Thomas. *The Pagan Temptation*. Grand Rapids: William B. Eerdmans, 1987.

Morohashi Tetsuji 諸橋轍次. *Daikanwa jiten* 大漢和辭典. 13 vols. Tokyo: Taishūkan shōten, 1957–1960.

Mungello, D. E. *Curious Land: Jesuit Accommodation and the Origins of Sinology*. Honolulu: University of Hawaii Press, 1989 reprint of 1985 publication.

———. "The Seventeenth-Century Jesuit Translation Project of the Confucian Four Books." In Ronan and Oh, pp. 252–272.

*New Catholic Encyclopedia*. New York: McGraw-Hill, 1967.

Nienhauser, William H., Jr., ed. *The Indiana Companion to Traditional Chinese Literature*. Bloomington: Indiana University Press, 1986.

Ōmura Seigai 大村西崖. *Bunjin gasen* 文人畫選. Tokyo: Tansei-sha, 1921–1922.

P'an Ching-cheng 潘景鄭, ed. *Chiang-yün-lou t'i-pa* 絳雲樓題跋 [Collected colophons of Ch'ien Ch'ien-i]. Shanghai: Chung-hua shu-chü, 1958.

P'an Lei 潘耒. *Sui-ch'u-t'ang chi* 邃初堂集. Edition dated 1710 in Library of Congress.

P'ang Yüan-chi 龐元濟. *Hsü-chai ming-hua lu* 虛齋名畫錄. 1909.

Peterson, Willard J. "Western Natural Philosophy Published in Late Ming China." *Proceedings of the American Philosophical Society* 117(4) (Aug. 1973):295–322.

———. "Why Did They Become Christians?—Yang T'ing-yün, Li Chih-tsao, and Hsü Kuang-ch'i." In Ronan and Oh, pp. 129–152.

Pfister, Louis, S.J. (1833–1891). *Notices Biographiques et Bibliographiques sur les Jésuites de l'Ancienne Mission de Chine*. Vol. 1. Kraus reprint, 1971, of 1932 Shanghai publication.

Ridder, Anne, ed. *Thomas Traherne: Poems, Centuries and Three Thanksgivings.* London: Oxford University Press, 1966.

Ronan, Charles E., S.J., and Bonnie B. C. Oh, eds. *East Meets West: The Jesuits in China, 1582–1773.* Chicago: Loyola University Press, 1988.

Rouleau, Francis A., S.J. "The First Chinese Priest of the Society of Jesus— Emmanuel de Siqueira (1633–73)." *Archivum Historicum Societatis Iesu* 28 (1959):3–50.

Shen Te-ch'ien 沈德潛 et al., eds. *Ch'ing-shih pieh-ts'ai chi* 清詩別裁集. 2 vols. Shanghai: Ku-chi ch'u-pan-she, 1984.

Shih Jun-chang 施閏章. *Shih Yü-shan hsien-sheng ch'üan chi* 施愚山先生全集. Edition of 1765.

*Shih-yung fo-hsüeh tz'u-tien* 實用佛學辭典. 2 vols. Hong Kong: Fo-ching liu-t'ung-ch'u, 1959 reprint.

Sirén, Osvald. *Chinese Painting: Leading Masters and Principles.* Vol. 7. London: Lund, Humphrics, 1956, 1958.

Smith, Joseph P., S.J., trans. *St. Irenaeus: Proof of the Apostolic Preaching.* New York and Ramsey: Newman Press, 1952.

Spence, Jonathan D. *The Question of Hu.* New York: Alfred A. Knopf, 1988.

Spence, Jonathan D., and John E. Wills, Jr., eds. *From Ming to Ch'ing: Conquest, Region, and Continuity in Seventeenth-Century China.* New Haven and London: Yale University Press, 1979.

Standaert, Nicholas. *Yang Tingyun, Confucian and Christian in Late Ming China.* Leiden: E. J. Brill, 1987.

Strassberg, Richard E. *The World of K'ung Shang-jen: A Man of Letters in Early Ch'ing China.* New York: Columbia University Press, 1983.

Struve, Lynne A. "Ambivalence and Action: Some Frustrated Scholars of the K'ang-hsi Period." In Spence and Wills, pp. 321–365.

Su Shih 蘇軾. *Tung-p'o ch'i chi* 東坡七集. In Ssu-pu pei-yao.

Sung Wan 宋琬. *An-ya-t'ang shih-chi* 安雅堂詩集. Ch'ing edition in Library of Congress.

Suzuki Kei 鈴木敬. *Comprehensive Illustrated Catalogue of Chinese Paintings.* 5 vols. Tokyo: University of Tokyo Press, 1982.

Tam, Laurence C. S. *Six Masters of Early Qing and Wu Li.* Hong Kong: Hong Kong Museum of Art, 1986.

T'an Cheng-pi 譚正璧. *Chung-kuo wen-hsüeh-chia ta tz'u-tien* 中國文學家大辭典. 2 vols. Taipei: Shih-chieh shu-chü reprint, 1971.

T'ang Pin 湯斌. *T'ang Tzu i-shu* 湯子遺書. Edition of 1870 in Library of Congress.

T'ang Shao-tsu 唐紹祖 et al., comp., *Ta Ch'ing lü-li* 大清律例.

T'ang Yü-chao 唐宇昭. *Ni kung-tz'u* 擬宮詞. In *Chieh-yüeh shan-fang hui-ch'ao* 借月山房彙鈔. 1812. Copy in library of the Jimbun Kagaku Kenkyū-jo, Kyoto University.

Temple, Lt.-Col. Sir Richard Carnac, ed. *The Travels of Peter Mundy in Europe and Asia, 1608–1667.* Vol. 3, pt. 1. London: Hakluyt Society, 1919.

Teng Chih-ch'eng 鄧之誠. *Ch'ing-shih chi-shih ch'u-pien* 清詩紀事初編. Shanghai: Ku-chi ch'u-pan-she, 1984; reprint of Chung-hua shu-chü publication of 1965, 2 vols.

*T'ien-hsüeh ch'uan-kai* 天學傳槩. Photostat in Library of Congress of copy in Vatican Biblioteca Apostolica.

Tomioka Masutarō 富岡益太郎. *Shi-Ō Go Un* 四王吳惲. Osaka: Hakubundō, 1919.

Wakeman, Frederic, Jr. *The Great Enterprise*. 2 vols. Berkeley: University of California Press, 1985.

Waley, Arthur. *The Book of Songs*. New York: Grove Press, n.d., reprint of 1937 publication.

Wall, John N., Jr., ed. *George Herbert: The Country Parson, The Temple*. New York: Paulist Press, Classics of Western Spirituality, 1981.

Wang Mou-lin 汪懋麟. *Pai-ch'ih-wu-t'ung-ko chi* 百尺梧桐閣集. Shanghai: Ku-chi ch'u-pan-she, 1980; photographic reprint of K'ang-hsi period edition, 3 vols.

Wang Shih-chen 王士禎. *Ch'ih-pei ou-t'an* 池北偶談. 2 vols. Peking: Chung-hua shu-chü, 1982.

———. *Yü-yang shan-jen chu-shu* 漁洋山人著述. K'ang-hsi period edition.

Wang Shih-min 王時敏. *Wang Feng-ch'ang shu hua t'i-pa* 王奉常書畫題跋. *T'ung-chou ou-po-lo shih*: 1910.

Wang Shih-yüan 汪士元. *Lu-yün-lou shu hua chi-lüeh* 麓雲樓書畫記略. Xeroxed copy, undated and unpaginated, Library of Freer and Sackler Galleries.

Wang Tsung-yen 汪宗衍. "*Wu Yü-shan 'Ao-chung tsa-yung' pu-shih*" 吳漁山嶴中雜詠補釋. In Chou K'ang-hsieh, pp. 141–146.

Wei Hsien 魏憲, ed. *Huang Ch'ing pai-ming-chia shih* 皇清百各家詩. Fu-ch'ing Wei-shih chen-chiang-t'ang 福清魏氏枕江堂. K'ang-hsi period edition.

*Wen hsüan* 文選. 2 vols. Hong Kong: Shang-wu yin-shu-kuan, 1960.

Whitfield, Roderick. *In Pursuit of Antiquity*. Princeton: Princeton University Art Museum, 1974.

Witek, John. W., S.J. Review of Chou K'ang-hsieh, *Wu Yü-shan yen-chiu lun-chi*. *Archivum Historicum Societatis Iesu* 44 (1975):186–188.

———. Review of Nicholas Standaert, *Yang Tingyun. Theological Studies* 50(2) (June 1989):369–371.

Wu Chih-chen 吳之振. *Huang-yeh-ts'un-chuang chi* 黃葉邨莊集. Edition of 1878 in Library of Congress.

Wu Chih-chen et al., eds. *Sung-shih ch'ao* 宋詩鈔. 4 vols. Peking: Chung-hua shu-chü, 1986.

Wu Li. See Chou K'ang-hsieh and Li Ti.

Wu Wei-yeh 吳偉業. *Wu Mei-ts'un shih-chi chien-chu* 吳梅村詩集箋注. 2 vols. Shanghai: Ku-chi ch'u-pan-she, 1983.

Yang Kuang-hsien 楊光先. *Pu-te-i* 不得已. Edition of 1929 in Library of Congress.

Yen Ling-feng 嚴靈峰. *Lieh Tzu chang-chü hsin-pien* 列子章句新編. Taipei: Wu-ch'iu-pei-chai, 1960.

Yu T'ung 尤侗. *Hsi-t'ang ch'üan chi* 西堂全集. K'ang-hsi period edition in Library of Congress.

————. *Yu T'ai-shih hsi-t'ang yü-chi* 尤太史西堂餘集. Edition of 1694 in Library of Congress.

Yuasa Yukihiko 湯淺幸孫. "*Sō-shi shō* no senja-tachi—hito ni yotte shi o sonsu" 「宋詩鈔」の選者たち—人によつて史を存す [the compilers of the *Sung-shih ch'ao:* comprehending history through men]. *Chūgoku bungaku hō* 中國文學報 20 (1965):68–92.

# Index

Note: There is no entry for Wu Li; for his individual works, see the Bibliography under Chou K'ang-hsieh and Li Ti, S.J.

## About the Author

Jonathan Chaves is professor of Chinese at The George Washington University in Washington, D.C. His books and articles have examined various aspects of Chinese poetry and its relation to the arts of calligraphy and painting. Among his publications are *Shisendō: The Hall of the Poetry Immortals* and *Pilgrim of the Clouds: Poems and Essays from Ming China by Yüan Hung-tao and His Brothers*, which was nominated for the National Book Award in Translation. Chaves' recent work explores the relation of later Chinese poetry to the philosophies and religions of China, especially Confucianism.